LIFE OF THE GOOD THIEF

LIFE OF THE GOOD THIEF

MSGR. GAUME
Protonotary Apostolic

Loreto Publications
2003

Published in 1882 by Burns & Oates

Published in 2003 by
Loreto Publications
P. O. Box 603
Fitzwilliam, NH 03447
www.LoretoPubs.org

ISBN: 1-930278-30-6

Printed and bound in the United States of America.

TABLE OF CONTENTS

TABLE OF CONTENTS *(CONTINUED)*

CHAPTER I

The Robbers of Judea

"And there were also two other malefactors, led with Him to be put to death. And when they were come to the place which is called Calvary, they crucified Him there: and the robbers, one on the right hand, and the other on the left. And Jesus said: Father, forgive them, for they know not what they do; but they, dividing his garments, cast lots. And the people stood beholding. And the rulers with them derided him, saying: He saved others: let him save himself, if he be Christ, the elect of God" (Lk 23:32-35).

"And one of those robbers who were hanged blasphemed him, saying: If thou be Christ, save thyself and us. But the other answering, rebuked him, saying: Neither dost thou fear God, seeing; thou art under the same condemnation? And we indeed justly: for we receive the due reward of our deeds. But this man hath done no evil. And he said to Jesus: Lord, remember me when thou shalt come into thy kingdom. And Jesus said to him: Amen I say to thee: This day thou shalt be with me in paradise" (Lk 23:39-43).

AMONG all the nations of antiquity highway robbery, we find, was reckoned as a capital offence. In the penal code of the Romans its punishment was crucifixion, at once the cruelest and the most shameful of deaths: "the reason of which," according to St. Gregory of Nyssa, was this — "that the robbers thus banded together did not shrink from murder as a means to their end. They even held themselves in readiness to do it (as was proved) by their choice of arms, supplies, and places of resort. Hence it was that they were subjected to the penalty thereof."[1]

The banditti of those times behaved pretty much in the same way as do their modern successors in such countries as are unhappily still infested by this scourge of society. They lived chiefly among the mountains, dwelling in caves, prowling about armed to the teeth, or lying in ambush near the highways, attacking the passers-by, robbing and stripping and wounding them, and often leaving them half dead. Well, indeed, for them if they were not killed outright. For proof of this deplorable state of things having existed in Judea at the time of our Lord, we have only to open the Gospel. We find it there in the parable of the man who went down from Jerusalem to Jericho. Nor is this the only place where robbers are spoken of in the sacred text. In the history of the Passion we find mention of Barabbas, a robber and a murderer. And again we read that two robbers suffered death together with the Son of God.

Some may wonder that the Gospel, usually so sparing of details, should make such frequent allusion to this class of evil-doers. It may appear surprising that our Lord should take, as the subject of one of his most beautiful parables, the incident of a man falling into their hands. But if we look into history, whether sacred or profane, the reason of this is quickly to be found. In Josephus and others we read that at this time, and until after the destruction of Jerusalem, the Holy Land was completely overrun with brigands. If, on the other hand, we consult the Holy Gospels, we see that our blessed Lord and Teacher was in the habit of adapting His lessons to the capacity of His hearers, and exemplifying His doctrines by reference to those things with which they were most familiar. Hence it was natural, if we may so speak, that, in a country infested by robbers, He should make use of such a parable as that of the Good Samaritan.

It may be interesting to note the causes of this so general lawlessness. They would appear to have been twofold. In the first place, the Jews, knowing themselves to be the chosen people of God, were ever impatient of all foreign yoke, and continually strove by all means in their power to throw it off. And in the next place, their alien rulers were at no pains to conciliate, but, on the contrary, cruelly oppressed them. The tyranny of the Syrian kings had been past bearing. The Roman rule was far milder, but still very galling to a free-minded people. A deep-seated feeling of hatred was continually fermenting in the hearts of the nation, and not infrequently broke out into street riots, and even open revolt. Quelled and dispersed by the soldiery, the rebels were still unsubdued. Driven out of the towns, they fled up into the mountains, and there, turning robbers, still continued to set the usurping authorities at defiance.

Herod I owed his reputation, and later on his throne, to his successful raids against these very brigands. Let us listen to the account of the struggle handed down to us by Josephus: "When Herod was still quite young, his father, Antipater, confided to him the government of Galilee, albeit he was only fifteen. But his youth was more than made up by his energy and courage. He soon found occasion for giving proof of these qualities. When Ezechias, a famous brigand chief, was laying waste the coast of Syria, he rose up suddenly, fell upon him, and slew him, together with a great number of his followers. This exploit gained him the love and esteem of the Syrians, whom the brigands had held in a sort of thraldom, and in every town and village he was praised and sung forth as the savior of the people, who had given them peace and security in the enjoyment of their goods. In this manner he came to be known to Sixtus Cæsar, kinsman to the great Cæsar, and at that time governor of Syria.[2]

But the evil was not put down for long. During Pilate's ten years of office, one of his chief difficulties lay in dealing with the brigands. And it was the same with his successors, Felix and Festus. When the former first came into the province, there was a very notorious robber-chief named Eleazar, who for twenty years had been the terror of the country. This was in the year of our Lord 51, the ninth of the reign of Claudius. Several expeditions had been made against him up into the mountains, but in vain; numbers of his men had been taken and executed; but Eleazar himself always contrived to escape. At last, force proving useless, Felix had recourse to treachery. He invited Eleazar to an interview, at the same time promising him protection and safety. But no sooner had the chief entered the governor's tent than he was seized, loaded with chains, and sent to Rome, where, in the Mamertine prison, he was made to suffer the death reserved for the worst of criminals.

But this ill-wreaked vengeance by no means stamped out the evil it was meant to deal with; far from it. Its only effect was to exasperate the surviving brigands, who now became more and more desperate. On all sides the country was laid waste, villages sacked and burnt, and their inhabitants put to the sword. Such was the pass to which things had come, when Festus succeeded Felix in the governorship of Judea, in the year of grace 58, second of the reign of Nero.[3]

Another cause of this deplorable state of affairs was the disaffection of the Jews of Cæsarea. The population of this town was mixed — part Jewish and part Syrian. For a long time all had been on a footing of perfect equality, enjoying the same rights, without distinction of race or religion. But during the reign of Nero, the Syrians, being jealous of the Jews, strove to deprive them of their right of citizenship. To this end the chief men among them wrote to Beryllus, who had been tutor to the Emperor, and bribed him with rich presents to obtain from his master the necessary permission. The imperial rescript had no sooner been obtained and published than the Jews to a man rose up in rebellion. A sort of guerilla warfare was waged in all the country round. Bands of brigands were organized in every part, and finally came together in the desert, under the command of a certain magician, who promised them entire success, which success was to be looked for through means of his pretended supernatural powers. To put an end to the civil war, Festus was obliged to send an army against the insurgents. And it was only after severe fighting that they were finally broken up, defeated, and slain.

Thus, these unhappy Jews, having rejected the promised Messias, were struck blind by the judgment of God, and ran after deceivers and set their faith on any liar. Having crucified

Him who is the very Truth, they were ready to risk their lives in defense of the wildest impostures. And so it always is. Whenever a nation or an age throws off the mild yoke of the Prince of Peace, and rises up against the Living Truth, so surely does it fall a prey to the spirit of war and strife — even the Father of Lies. And if God intervene not in some special and striking manner, the world thus blinded falls from error into error, escaping tyranny only to destroy itself by anarchy, and finally becoming the victim of some needy adventurer or barbaric chief.

From the foregoing historic details the reader will have gathered some notion of the disorganized state of society in Judea at the time of our Lord, and will have seen how very probable it is that the two thieves who suffered with Christ on Calvary may have belonged to one of these bands of brigands.[4] Hence he will find no difficulty in accepting the ancient and well-established tradition of which we are about to speak.

CHAPTER 2

Traditions Concerning the Good Thief

THE Massacre of the Innocents was about to take place. Hundreds of these little victims were destined to perish that One Child might not escape. But God laughs to scorn the counsels of evil men, and vainly shall the kings rage against Him and against His Anointed. Herod gained nothing by his wholesale barbarity save the curses of posterity; for "being warned in sleep by an angel, Joseph took the Child and His mother by night, and fled with them into Egypt" (Mt 2:11-14).

There are two ways of going from Bethlehem down to Egypt — the land route, and that by sea. Now, to reach the nearest port it is necessary to come by Joppa, across sixty miles of a densely-inhabited country. This would have been to run the risk of discovery and arrest. Besides, even had the fugitives arrived safely at the place of embarkation, they would probably have had several days to wait before a ship set sail, and every hour was full of danger. Finally, money would be required to pay the passage. Now, the Holy Family were very poor at this time, perhaps more so than usual. They had to start on their journey unprepared, in the middle of the night. The unexpected command had been sent from Heaven. Without a moment's hesitation, Joseph had obeyed, and gone forth, probably without purse or scrip. These, and other reasons, incline us to think that the sea route was not the one chosen. If our surmise be correct, the Holy Family must have journeyed overland. This also had its dangers. Between the southern frontier of Judea and the land of Egypt there stretches a large tract of desert, extending for 120 miles. We have already seen that Palestine was infested on every side by brigands. Much more would they be likely to be found in these wild, uninhabited places, where they would be in a position to stop and pillage caravans without fear of detection.

Tradition is unanimous on the subject of this journey. Its faithful mouthpiece, Christian art, always represents the flight as taking place overland, St. Joseph leading an ass on which is seated the Virgin Mother, holding her child in her arms. Another tradition, which is found in Oriental documents as old as the third century, tells us that the Holy Family did not escape the common peril, but fell into the hands of brigands. This incident had so much influence on the life of the Good Thief, St. Dismas,* that, before relating it, it may be as well to give what proof we have of its authenticity.

That the Holy Family should have been surprised by robbers during the flight into Egypt has, in itself, nothing incredible. On the contrary, the historic details given above serve to show that it was probable, nay, almost inevitable. It is true that no mention is made of the event in the Holy Gospels; but this silence of the sacred writers is no proof that it did not take place. The New Testament is far from recording every incident of our Savior's life. St. John tells us that if all these things were written, the world would not be able to contain all the books so produced. (Jn 21:25) There are even most important points left unnoticed, such, for instance, as the substitution of the Sunday for the Jewish Sabbath, and the validity of baptism by infusion. But when the Holy Scriptures are silent, the voice of tradition makes itself heard. From the very earliest times this tradition was taken down in writing. We learn from St. Luke that even in his day much had already been written. (Lk 1:1) Nor is this surprising, when we consider the multitudes

---

* The author originally used the name "Dimas" instead of "Dismas", as the saint is more commonly called. The name has been changed to Dismas throughout the book for the convenience of the reader. — Ed. note

that flocked to Palestine from every part of the known world for the sake of seeing and hearing the Son of God, and being cured of their infirmities.[1] Man has an inborn love of the marvelous, and we cannot suppose that these pilgrims, on their return home, were silent concerning the wonders they had seen and heard; they doubtless published them abroad, by writing as well as by word of mouth. Thus we can easily account for the origin of the many versions of our Lord's life to which the Evangelist refers.

These first writings have unfortunately all perished, but much of their matter may be found in documents still extant, which, at comparatively early date, were widely circulated both in East and West. Many of these, it must be confessed, were written with more piety than wisdom. Others, again, were composed by heretics, who tainted them with an admixture of their own special errors. None of them were really composed by those whose names they bear. Hence the Church, in her unerring wisdom, has not suffered them to be incorporated in the sacred canon.

Yet although declaring these writings apocryphal, the Church has never pronounced them to be altogether false. Much good grain is there, though not unmixed with chaff. There is one test by which they are easily sifted — the question whether or not they are in conformity with the authorized versions. When the details they suggest are not contrary to the teaching of the Church, to Faith, or to sound reason, but rather appear probable, from their being in keeping with ancient usages and customs, they may safely be considered as a sort of supplementary tradition, which neither has been, nor can be, condemned.

The Church herself has not disdained to make use of these writings in her controversies with her rebellious children. One of them — the famous letter to Abgarus — although declared apocryphal by Pope Gelasius, was referred to in the following terms by St. Gregory II, when writing to the iconoclastic emperor, Leo the Isaurian: "When Christ was in the neighborhood of Jerusalem, Abgarus, who was at that time King of Edessa, having heard of the fame of His miracles, wrote to Him, and received in answer a letter written by the Lord himself, together with a portrait of His sacred and most glorious countenance. Send, therefore, and go thyself, and behold this likeness not made with hands. Thither do the multitudes of the East draw nigh and pray."[2]

And later on, another Pope, Adrian I, in recounting to Charlemagne what passed at the council held at Rome, in the year 709, says: "Our predecessor, the Lord Stephen, of holy memory, who as Pope presided over the said Council, brought forward much true testimony, which he himself confirmed, teaching also that we must not omit or disregard those things which have been made known to us by the faithful of the East. That they should not be mentioned in the Holy Gospel is in no way surprising, for does not the Evangelist himself say, 'Many other things did Jesus which are not written in this book?' Wherefore we may receive their witness, that as the time of the Passion was approaching, the Savior of mankind wrote a letter to Abgarus, King of Edessa, who had written to him expressing his desire to see Him and to provide Him with an abode, where He should be safe from the persecution of the Jews." Then follows the letter, given in full.[3]

We must observe that these letters of St. Gregory and of Pope Adrian were official documents addressed to princes, one of whom was the avowed foe of holy images. Can we suppose that Popes would have brought forward such writings as the letter of Abgarus, and our Lord's answer to it, as evidence in favor of the veneration of images, unless they carried great weight in the eyes of all?

Certain modern Catholic critics are too much inclined to despise all the apocryphal writings. They might profitably learn a lesson on this subject from the great Anglican writers. Pearson, among others, has a passage upon the letter to Abgarus, as cited by Eusebius, wherein he fully accepts the tradition handed down. His comments do as much honor to his fairness and impartiality, as to his learning.[4]

The wise and learned historian, Baronius, did not hesitate to rely upon the authority of the apocryphal Gospels to prove — as against St. Jerome — that the Zacharias put to death by the Jews between the temple and the altar, was the same Zacharias who was the father of St. John the Baptist. The great annalist lays down an excellent rule, which all should follow in regard to these writings. He says they should be accepted with prudence and reserve — "*caute admittenda;*" and not too strenuously defended — "*mordicus defendi non debent.*"[5] It is unnecessary for me to add that I have adhered scrupulously to this rule throughout the course of this work.

I must now give a few words from Brunet on this subject. He says: "The incidents and circumstances recorded in the apocryphal Gospels have not failed to bear fruit. For several hundred years they exercised a most powerful and beneficial influence on the development of art and poetry. During the Middle Ages, epics, mysteries, painting and sculpture all found in them motives for some of their best and highest efforts. To neglect the study of the apocryphal Gospels would be to renounce all hope of discovering the clue to the real meaning of Christian art; for in them is to be found the source whence, ever since the downfall of paganism, art has drawn its endless symbolism. Certain circumstances handed down in these legends have been immortalized by the brush of the great masters of the Italian school, and have suggested symbols and types which are now every day reproduced by artists of all kinds."[6]

Of these apocryphal writings it is only necessary for our purpose to single out two. The one gives us a detailed account of the meeting of the Holy Family with the robbers of the desert. The other has preserved to us the names of the two thieves crucified on Calvary. The most ancient is called the "Gospel of the Holy Childhood,"[7] which dates as far back as the end of the second century. It was first written in Syriac or Greek, and thence translated into the different languages of both East and West. It has been found in Egypt, among the Copts; in India, among the Christians of the coasts of Malabar; in Armenia, and even among the Mussulmen. In Europe, it has been widely circulated, many editions having been published in almost every language.[8]

By whomsoever this Gospel may have been written, it contains facts about which there can be no doubt, such, for instance, as the Adoration of the Magi, and the reason of the Flight into Egypt. In the seventh chapter it is said, "This is what came to pass. When the Lord Jesus was born at Bethlehem, a town of Judea, in the reign of King Herod, wise men came from the land of the East, according to the prediction of Zoroaster, and they brought with them presents, gold, incense, and myrrh, and they worshipped the Child, and offered Him their gifts."[9]

And in the ninth chapter: "Herod, seeing that the wise men returned not to him, began to consider in his mind how he should put the Lord Jesus to death. Then an angel appeared to Joseph in his sleep, and said to him, Arise, take the child and His mother, and fly with them into Egypt. And, at cock-crow, Joseph arose and fled."

This Gospel also contains facts belonging to, what we may call, tradition of the second order. To this category belongs the following history. It is in the twenty-third chapter:

"And, presently, they came to the entrance of the desert. And, hearing that it was infested by robbers, they determined to cross it, during the night. But, suddenly, they perceived two robbers, who were lying near them, asleep, and round about were many other robbers, their associates, and they also were asleep.

"The names of these two robbers were Titus and Dumachus.[10] The first said to the other, 'I beg thee, let these travelers go in peace, lest our comrades discover them.' And Dumachus refused. Whereon Titus said to him: 'I beseech thee, accept of me, forty drachmas, and take my belt as security.' And he, offering it, implored him not to call their comrades or give the alarm.

"Mary, seeing this robber so well inclined towards her, said to him, 'May God uphold thee with His right hand, and grant thee the remission of thy sins.'

"And the Lord Jesus said to his mother, 'In thirty years' time, O my mother, the Jews will crucify Me, and these two robbers shall be crucified with Me, Titus on my right hand and Dumachus on my left, and behold, that day, Titus shall be with me in Paradise.'

"And when He had thus spoken, His mother answered Him, saying, 'God forbid that such things should befall Thee.' And they went on their way towards the city of idols."

But, the most important of all the Apocryphal writings, is the Gospel of Nicodemus. Hardly a sentence of it, but what is reproduced by many of the early fathers, such as St. Cyril of Jerusalem, St. Chrysostom, Firmicus Maternus, and St. Hippolytus, so that its general sense is unimpeachable. It has been much read in the West, where it was known from a very early period. In its present form it is attributed to the fourth or fifth century.

Gregory of Tours, Vincent of Beauvais, and many other writers of the Middle Ages, frequently quote this Gospel, without ever expressing any doubt as to its authenticity. Eusebius of Alexandria analyzed, and wrote a commentary upon it, and showed no scruple in accepting its authority. At no very distant time, the Gospel of Nicodemus was regularly read in the Greek Church, not, it is true, as forming part of the sacred canon, but as being a work full of edification, written by a holy and venerable man. It is impossible to say how many editions it has gone through. They are innumerable.

Like the Gospel of the Holy Childhood, that of Nicodemus records, over and above those events of which the New Testament gives us divine testimony, certain other incidents and details not mentioned by the Evangelists, in their brief narrative.

We will content ourselves with citing a single passage, which throws a light upon the subject of our history. It is from the tenth chapter:

"And Jesus went forth from the Praetorium. And when He had reached the place called Golgotha, the soldiers took off, from Him, His own garment, and girded Him with a linen cloth, and put, upon His Head, a crown of thorns and a reed in His hands; and they crucified with Him two thieves, Dismas on His right hand, and Gestas on His left."

There are numerous passages in the works of the fathers in which mention is made both of the names of the two thieves and of their encounter with the Holy Family in the desert. The good faith as well as the discrimination of these writers being established beyond doubt, it matters little whether their information was derived from the above-mentioned documents, or from others which have long since perished.

Among the published works of St. Augustine is a treatise, entitled De Vita Eremitica. Until lately it was attributed to the great Bishop of Hippo. We ourselves are more inclined to the opinion of the learned Père Raynaud, who believes it to have been written by St. Anselm, Archbishop of Canterbury. But, whoever the author, the work is undoubtedly old and of much weight. We quote it as confirming the tradition of which we have been speaking.

"Consider as true that tradition, which represents the Holy Family as falling into the hands of robbers and owing their deliverance to a young man who was the son of their chief. The legend is that, being on the point of rifling them, he suddenly caught sight of the Divine Infant, resting in His mother's arms. He was struck with awe on beholding the glorious beauty and majesty of His countenance, and believed at once that He was something more than man, and burning with love, he embraced Him, saying: 'O most Blessed of children, if ever a time should come when I should crave Thy mercy, remember me and forget not what has passed this day.'

"The same tradition goes on to say that this young man was the same as the thief, who was crucified on Christ's right hand. And he, turning towards the Lord, recognized in Him the glorious Infant whose majesty he had seen long since, and, being mindful of his prayer, he said to Him: 'Lord, remember me when Thou comest to thy kingdom.'

"This tradition is, I think, far from useless as an incentive to love of God, but it should be cited without too bold or positive affirmation."[11]

The learned Cardinal, St. Peter Damian, who died in the year 1072, attributed the conversion of the Good Thief to the prayers of the Blessed Virgin, who had recognized in him the young man who had protected her son in the desert.[12] I say protected, because not only had he prevented the Holy Family from being robbed by his comrades, but he had made them pass the night in his own dwelling, and the next day provided them with all that was necessary for their journey, the safety of which he insured by sending with them an armed escort.

It would take too long to enumerate all those writers, distinguished alike for learning and holiness, who, without doubt or hesitation, have become the exponents of this tradition. We will content ourselves, therefore, with the following brief quotations from a few of those best known.

The blessed James of Voragine, Archbishop of Genoa, thus mentions the legend in one of his sermons: "During their flight into Egypt the Holy Family fell into the hands of robbers. One of them, ravished by the beauty of the Child, said to his companions: 'Verily I say to you that if it were possible for God to assume our nature I should believe this Child to be God.' His companions were so much softened by these words that they allowed the Child and his mother to depart unhurt."[13]

The learned Bishop of Equilium, Peter de Natalibus, adds the following details: "Not only did the young robber abstain from plundering the Child and his mother, but so touched was he by their beauty, that he begged of them to stay the night with him, he ministering unto them, and afterwards guarded them with an armed escort to the end of their journey."[14]

The great Landolphus of Saxony, in his admirable Life of Christ, also makes mention of this meeting with the robbers. It is, perhaps, unnecessary to give the quotation, as it is couched in almost exactly the same terms as that already cited from St. Anselm. (De Vita Eremitica, cited above.)[15]

We may also name the pious and learned Padre Orilia, who, having carefully studied the question, accepts the tradition as beyond reasonable doubt. He says: "I might make a long list of the writers who give testimony to these things, but it seems to me superfluous."[16]

We must add that in the East this tradition is received without doubt or hesitation, by Greeks and Latins alike.

One word on the slight variations to be found in the different accounts. We do not think they are considerable enough in any way to invalidate the main points of the tradition. There is hardly a passage in history, whether sacred or profane, which has not been recorded by various writers in divers forms. It is, indeed, unavoidable that there should be slight variations, and even, sometimes, apparent contradictions, but, where these do not touch the essential parts of the event so recorded, even the severest criticism lets them pass.

We must not leave unnoticed a proof (of the moral order) furnished by the agreement of this tradition with what we so often find to be the working of the providence of God. His infinite knowledge includes all things, whether past, present, or to come, and His goodness knows no bounds. The Gospel tells us of many instances where meetings with our Lord were fruitful of grace and salvation. May we not suppose that the providence of God had more influence in bringing them about than a mere blind chance? It was not surely to accident that the Samaritan woman, Zaccheus, Matthew, and others owed their conversion, or the man possessed by the legion of devils, his cure. Blind, indeed, is he who does not see in these events the working of the providence of God — His mercy seeking out the sinner, whom Christ had come to save.

We therefore do not hesitate to impute the meeting in the desert to the same divine cause, and to believe that He, Who has said: "I was a stranger and you took Me in," and Who has promised that neither this, nor even a cup of cold water should go without its reward; that He, in His mercy, designed, through this meeting and the good deed it gave occasion for, to implant in the soul of the young robber a seed of grace, which should one day produce fruit of salvation. Thus we admire on Calvary a conversion prepared many years beforehand, and draw hence much comfort for such as seem to be hopelessly sunk in sin, and to have let pass the accepted time. Ay, there is hope for all, and the Day of Salvation may be at the door while yet we sorrow, thinking it afar off.

CHAPTER 3

Name and Origin of the Good Thief

WE do not find in the Holy Gospel either the name or the origin of the Good Thief. His previous history, like that of many other Biblical characters, is shrouded in silence. But although the sun denies us his light, we are not altogether left in darkness. The perfect light of revelation may, to some extent, be replaced by what we may call the torchlight of tradition. When the one fails us, we must look to the other, whereby to guide our path. Let us, therefore, have recourse for information to the writings of the fathers.

St. Chrysostom says, in speaking of what passed on Calvary: "The man to whom these words were spoken was a robber — one ignorant of the sublime truths of religion, knowing nothing of the prophecies, who had spent all his life in desert places, committing many murders, never hearing the Word of God, or being present at the reading of the Holy Scriptures."[1]

St. Augustine speaks in the same sense: "Until now, this robber had not known Christ. Had he known him, who can say but that he, who was the first to enter the Kingdom, might perchance have been ranked as not the least among the Apostles?"[2]

Also Eusebius, who says: "Before this he had known neither religion nor Christ."[3]

Now it does not seem possible that a Jew, however abandoned and lawless, could be so wholly ignorant of the religion of his nation as never to have heard of the Law, or the Prophets, or the looked-for Messias. Hence we conclude that the Good Thief must have been a pagan. This seems to be also the sentiment of St. Chrysostom, as may be gathered from the following passage:

"There were crucified two thieves — types of Jews and Gentiles. The penitent thief is the type of the people gathered from the Gentiles, who, having walked in error, now accept the truth. But that other, who unto the end remains an unconverted thief, he is the type of the Jews. Until the time of the crucifixion they had walked together in the way of sin, but the cross has separated them thenceforth."[4]

It being proved from patristic evidence, that the Good Thief was by birth a Gentile, there comes the question as to where he was born. We know that on all sides Palestine was surrounded by idolatrous nations — to which of them did he belong? Did he first see the light in the desert, in a robber's cave, or in some town or village? To this question, tradition gives no clear answer. It has only preserved to us the memory of the place which was the chief scene of his misdeeds.

The following description is taken from the valuable work of the learned Quaresmus, Notary Apostolic for the Holy Land:

"On leaving Rama, the pilgrims journey in an easterly direction towards the Holy City, which is distant about thirty miles. With the exception of the Valley of Rama, which is very beautiful and fertile, and extends about eight miles, the rest of the country is mountainous, rugged, and barren, very difficult of access. Ten miles beyond Rama — about half a mile from the main road — may be seen the ruins of a hamlet, situated on the summit of a hill. Formerly there was a fine church there, but there is very little of it now standing. This heap of ruins goes by the name of the 'Village of the Good Thief.' But it is by no means certain that the Good Thief was born here. Tradition only says that the ruined church was built in his honor."[5]

Thus wrote, in the seventeenth century, one of the most accurate historians of the Holy Land. We will now give the testimony of a distinguished contemporary author, Msgr. Mislin, which proves once again that in the unchanging East nothing perishes, be it ruin or tradition:

"After leaving Rama the road leads, for about two hours, over broken and stony ground, until it reaches the first pass of the mountains of Judea. There one comes upon a few tenanted huts, and above, situated on a hill, are the ruins of Latroun, said to have been the home of the Good Thief. It was destroyed by Saladin, as also the castles of Plans and Mai, after the destruction of Joppa, Rama, and Ascalon.

"These ruins, the aspect of which is in keeping with their reputation, were much more formidable a few years back than they are now. They served as a place of resort for brigands, who had inherited from the Good Thief the traditions of his life, if not of his repentance. Ibrahim put an end to their depredations and destroyed their stronghold, and, under his rule travelers were safe. But when the Pashas from Constantinople came back to their possessions, the brigands of Latroun and other places also returned to theirs, and are now established there in good force."[6]

Of what race was the Good Thief — Arab, Phœnician, or Syrian? The common opinion is that he was an Egyptian. Quaresmus says: "From the authors I have consulted it would appear that the Good Thief was an Egyptian, and consequently that he was born, not in Judea, but in Egypt, so that the village, which bears his name, cannot have been his birthplace. However this may be, it is certain that the inhabitants of this village had for him a special devotion, and raised a church in his honor."

The learned Bishop of Equilium affirms the same thing: "This robber was by birth an Egyptian, as we read in St. John Damascene. At the time of our Lord's flight into Egypt, he and his associates lived by pillaging travelers."[7]

Padre Orilia, after examining the question, sums up in these words: "From the unanimous testimony of the above-mentioned writers, we may conclude, with moral certainty, that the Good Thief belonged to the Egyptian nation."[8]

If this be so, then must he have been sunk in the grossest idolatry the world had ever seen. He must have been a worshipper of all kinds of serpents, of the dragon of Meteli, of the ram of Mendez, of crocodiles, of cats, of oxen, and finally of leeks and onions — of everything, in a word, which is most vile and disgusting. Ah! let us measure, if we can, the distance between this abyss of degradation and the height of Calvary, and then we shall be able to understand the greatness of that miracle which, in the twinkling of an eye, changed this abandoned robber into a great saint.

We find no clue as to the name of the Good Thief in any writings anterior to the end of the second century. After that date the name generally given, both in East and West, is Dismas. In the Gospel of Nicodemus we find the following passage: "Pilate ordered that the reason of his condemnation should be written on a board, in Hebrew, and Greek, and Latin characters: 'This is the King of the Jews.' And Gestas, one of the robbers who was crucified with Him, said to Jesus: 'If Thou art the Christ deliver both Thyself and us.' But Dismas, answering, rebuked him, saying: 'Hast thou no fear of God, thou, who also art condemned.' "[9]

In his Catalogue of Saints, Peter de Natalibus gives the same names. "About the time of our Lord's death, Dismas and another robber, Gestas by name, had been apprehended by the Jews on account of their crimes. These, likewise, were condemned to death."[10]

The learned Archbishop of Genoa, James of Voragine, when preaching to his people, speaks in these terms: "The young robber, who persuaded his comrades to let the Holy Family go in peace, was named Dismas."[11]

The great Spanish theologian, Salmeron, also adopts the names given in the Apocrypha. He says: "The names of these robbers, according to Nicodemus, were Dismas and Gestas, two of the most famous brigands of their time," etc.[12]

In Italy we find the same name preserved. Masimo, in his Bologna Illustrata, writes that "St. Dismas, the Good Thief, is honored in the Church of St. Vitalis and Agricola, where is preserved a portion of his cross."

Quaresmus repeats the same tradition. He says: "In the ancient martyrologies the Good Thief, whose memory is before God, is called Dismas. We find the same name in William Pipinus, *Statione* 7a *Christi Patientis*, and in Ravisius, *Officinæ,* t. i. tit *De Cruce*. They also teach that he was of the Egyptian nation."[13]

The celebrated Maurolyeo, the predecessor of Baronius, in the revision of the Martyrology, does not hesitate to insert in it the name of St. Dismas, and he is considered a great authority, and is quoted on this point by the Bollandists themselves without adverse comment.[14]

We find the same name in the writings of Théophile Raynaud, Godefroy de Vendôme, Malonio, Padre Orilia, Blessed Simon of Cassia, the learned Spanish theologian Sylveira, and many others.[15]

In Baronius' corrected version of the Roman Martyrology, we find for the 25th of March: "At Jerusalem — commemoration of the Good Thief, who confessed Christ on the Cross, and de-served to hear from Him those words: 'This day shalt thou be with Me in Paradise.'" The Cardinal adds in a note, "He is gen-erally called Dismas, but this name is not inserted in the Martyrology, doubtless because it is taken from the Apocryphal Gospels. Nevertheless, we find good number of churches dedicated to the Good Thief, under the invocation of this name."

We must remember that this was written in the sixteenth century, when it was necessary to conciliate as much as possible the carping and fault-finding spirit of the times, and to give the Protestant critics nothing which they might legitimately take exception to. For this same reason, the name Dismas was suppressed when permission was given to certain of the religious orders to recite the Office of the Good Thief. This was done by Sixtus V in favor of the Order of Mercy in the sixteenth century; by the Congregation of Rites in 1724, at the time of the founding of the *Pii Operai* (Congregation of Devout Workmen); and again when the same faculty was given to the canons regular of St. Gaetano.

The wise discretion of Rome on this point does not, in my opinion, in any way invalidate the tradition of which I have been speaking. It is true that it is founded on the Apocrypha, but every one admits that the Apocrypha contains much truth. The authorities we have already quoted prove this sufficiently. In this particular case the tradition has been adopted by almost all the ecclesiastical writers — "*plerique*," to use the expression of Baronius — and besides it has been acted upon in Italy and elsewhere by the faithful, who have built numberless churches under the invocation of Saint Dismas.

It seems to me that to reject this name would be to accuse of imprudent hastiness all those venerable men who, century after century, have handed it down to us; therefore we shall always in this book make use of the name of Dismas, whenever we have occasion to speak of the glorious convert of Mount Calvary.

Moreover, a slight knowledge of the customs of the ancients shows us that the names of the two thieves must have been matter of public notoriety. In our time there is no public announcement of the names of criminals at the moment of their execution, nor yet any writing them up on placards or otherwise, yet every one knows who they are. But in the old times there was, besides the trial, another, and more solemn, means of proclaiming them.

Now with the Jews, as with the Romans, the custom was that a herald should walk before the criminal on the way to execution, proclaiming his name the while, or else that it should be written in large letters on a board hung round his neck during the funeral procession, and afterwards placed on the gibbet, above the sufferer's head.

Thus it was with our Lord. As we read in the Gospel, His adorable name was written upon the cross in three languages. We do not know whether the board on which it was inscribed was fixed upon the cross in the Prætorium or only upon Calvary, in which latter case it must have been carried before Him all the way. However this may be, it was placed above His head at the time of the crucifixion. Many, perhaps, of those who were come up to Jerusalem for the Paschal Feast, thus learnt, for the first time, the name and rank of the august Victim.

In the same way, all Jerusalem, and the strangers there assembled, must have known with certainty the names of the two thieves, for what was done to our Lord was nowise exceptional. Let us listen to the testimony of the learned Justus Lipsius.

In speaking of death by crucifixion, he says: "When the criminal was fastened to the cross the inscription was then put up. It set forth the crime of which the execution was the punishment. It was the custom to carry this inscription before the criminal or to make him carry it himself."[16]

This statement of Justus Lipsius is founded upon history, and may be applied to all forms of criminal execution. Suetonius tells us the following revolting anecdote about Caligula. "At Rome, during a public feast, a slave having dropped a plate of silver on one of the couches, Caligula at once commanded the executioner to cut off his hands, and to suspend them round his neck, hanging down on to his breast, and thus to lead him round the assembled guests, preceded by an inscription setting forth the cause of his punishment."[17]

Domitian did not fall far short of Caligula in cruelty, while, like him, conforming to the general usage in this respect. He was one day celebrating the public games, when a veteran of the Parmularians ventured to indulge in a jest. The man was the father of a family, and only took advantage of the freedom of speech granted to the soldiery. Seeing that one of the gladitors, by race a Thracian, was of poor and mean appearance, he said: "This Thracian is but a *mermillo,* and hardly worthy of him who provides the games." Upon which, Domitian, believing his own divine majesty to be insulted, ordered the unfortunate veteran to be thrown to the dogs. But previously he had put upon him his cause: "This Parmularian spoke impiously."[18]

Not only was the criminal's name written and proclaimed, but bells were rung and trumpets blown to attract more attention. Tacitus says, speaking of a famous execution: "When the consuls had conducted Publius Martius outside the Esquiline gate, they caused the trumpet to be sounded, and the criminal to be executed, according to the ancient custom."[19] Seneca, in describing an execution, speaks in these terms: "The prætor ascends his tribunal; the people stand expectant. The criminal's hands are then tied behind his back. All look sadly on, while the herald proclaims silence, and reads the motive of condemnation as is ordered by the law. And now resound the trumpets."

This custom was universal, throughout the Roman empire. No criminal was ever put to death without having his cause proclaimed, either by means of the herald or the placard. Hence the proverb: *"Hunc vel illum, hoc illove titulo delatum ad judicem."*[20]

Spartian tells us that when Septimus Severus was appointed Proconsul of Africa, one of the members of the municipality of Leptis, who had formerly been his schoolfellow, came to meet him in State, preceded by torch-bearers, and ventured to embrace him, although himself a plebeian; upon which the proud patrician ordered him to be beaten with rods, a herald proclaiming the while: "Plebeian, be not so insolent as to embrace the legate of the Roman people."[21]

In the Life of Alexander Severus, we find evidence of this same custom of proclamation. It is there recorded that a certain courtier, named Vetronius Surinus, pretended to have a great influence over the Emperor, and to be able to obtain from him whatever he would. All who had any favor to ask for, addressed themselves to this man, and brought him rich presents, which he quietly accepted, but without presenting their petitions to the prince. At last the fraud was discovered, and Surinus was condemned to be suspended on a cross over a slow fire of straw and damp wood, and choked by the smoke, so that as the herald meanwhile proclaimed: "He, who sold smoke, is now punished by the smoke."[22] In an edict of the Emperor Severus, and in another of Antoninus Pius, we find the following words: "Whosoever shall perjure himself, swearing by the genius of his prince, shall be beaten with rods, these words being repeatedly called out the while: "Learn not to perjure thyself."

Tertullian makes mention of this custom as having been observed in regard to the Christians, whose sentences, he says, were their praise.[23]

St. Ambrose, in speaking of the martyrdom of St. Agnes, says: "The judge ordered that she should be taken to the Emperor, preceded by the herald making proclamation: 'This is Agnes, a sacrilegious virgin, guilty of blasphemy against the gods, for which she is condemned to the Lupanar.'"

Eusebius speaks of the same usage as being in force at Lyons, during the persecutions. When the glorious martyr, Altalus, was exposed in the amphitheatre, a placard was borne before him with the words "This is Altalus, the Christian."[24] In other places the Christian's cause ran thus: "*Imperatorum et deorum inimicus.*"[25]

In the changeless East, we find the same custom still in use. In the province of Tonkin, in Cochin China, and Korea, our saintly missionaries are even now led to death preceded by a placard on which are written their names and cause. Many of these may be seen at Paris at the Seminaire des Missions Étrangères, where they are kept as relics.

It may not be uninteresting to give here one or two of these inscriptions. We will first mention that of M. Schoeffler, who was martyred on the 1st of May, 1851. It is as follows: "Notwithstanding that the religion of Jesus is severely proscribed, this Augustine, an European priest, has dared to come here secretly for the sake of preaching it and seducing the people.

On being arrested, he has confessed everything. His guilt is manifest. Therefore, the said Augustine is condemned to have his head out off and thrown into the river."[26] These words were written on a small placard and carried like a banner before the martyr's face.

In the 236th number of the *Annals of the Propagation of the Faith* we find the account of a martyrdom which took place in Korea, in 1866. The sufferers were Msgr. Berneux, and MM. de Bretenières, Beaulieu, and Doric. On being led out of prison, they were seated, each one in a sort of chair carried by two men. To this their hands and feet were tied, and their heads thrown back and caught by the hair. Thus they went to the place of execution, looking up to Heaven, whither they were wending. At the back of their heads was fixed the placard, on both sides of which was written in large letters: "Rebel and breaker of the law, condemned to death after undergoing many torments."

The same custom was observed a few days later, when the venerable Peter Tjoi was put to death by crucifixion.

CHAPTER 4

The Good Thief's Manner of Life

IT is not possible to draw pure water from a poisoned source, neither can a tree produce good fruit if its root be withered. But, if such a phenomenon were to occur, we should call it a miracle. The same law obtains in the moral, as in the physical world. The proverb, "Like father, like son," is true on the whole, and the cases in which it is not verified are exceptional.

In our inquiries into the life and condition of St. Dismas, our first question, therefore, concerns his father. The answer to this is to be found in the "Vita Eremitica," the authority of which is undoubted, however much its authorship may be questioned.

Therein we find that the father of the Good Thief was a brigand chief. Among brigands the posts of command are held by those who are possessed of courage, coolness, strength, and cunning, together with sufficient cruelty and cupidity for the full indulgence of rapine and murder. In a word, a chief of brigands must be a sort of incarnation of wickedness.

Such must have been the father of Dismas, and the son was like him. Born probably in one of the caves of the wilderness, he grew up and spent his life among robbers. St. Chrysostom says of him that he spent all his time in the desert, and, in saying this, he is only, as it were, the mouthpiece of tradition. In the desert, his only intercourse with his fellow men would be criminal in the last degree. His profession would force him to rob all who came in his way, and, in case of resistance, to murder them. Sometimes he would fight in self-defence; then, again, for purposes of revenge;[1] and always he would have, as an incentive to fresh crimes, his ambition, which would urge him to rival, if not to surpass, his father, so as one day to succeed him as chief. Bad motives, therefore, were not wanting, nor yet the occasion for acting upon them. According to St. Ambrose, he made free use of both, and became guilty of the most atrocious crimes, for which at last he was put to death, after confessing his guilt.[2] St. Leo and St. Chrysostom specify some of his crimes. They speak of robberies, housebreaking, and murders. St. Chrysostom ends up by saying that he was sunk in the lowest depths of corruption and wickedness.[3]

To all this St. Gregory the Great adds the guilt of fratricide. "It is well," he says, "to keep before our eyes the example of this thief, who from the lowest deep of sin ascends the cross, and thence enters Paradise. Let us consider what was his state on coming to the place of execution, and what, on leaving it. He comes guilty of blood, even his brother's blood; but on the cross he is changed, by the power of grace. And he, who killed his brother, now bears witness to the undying life of his expiring Lord, by the words: 'Remember me, when Thou shalt come into Thy kingdom.'"[4]

St. Eulogius endorses the same accusation. He says: "What obstacle did it prove to the conversion of the thief in the Gospel, that he mounted the cross with hands stained by his brother's blood? Even in the throes of death was he not made illustrious by the most striking miracles? He who had spent his whole life in deeds of pillage and rapine — he, even he, in one instant of repentance, was not only cleansed from every stain of guilt, but was made worthy to accompany the Savior, and thus to be the first to enter Paradise, according to the words of our Lord: 'This day shalt thou be with Me in Paradise.'"[5]

This last crime of fratricide speaks volumes. Of what was he not capable, who, trampling on the most sacred family ties, dared even slay his brother? We are not surprised that Eusebius, in speaking of this new Cain, should characterize him as a most atrocious criminal, covered all over with guilt.[6]

The testimony of the fathers is confirmed by the very sentence which Dismas underwent. Death by crucifixion was at once the most cruel and the most degrading of all punishments, and was reserved for the worst and most infamous crimes. Hence it was, as St. Chrysostom remarks, that the Jews chose to inflict this death upon our Lord, for the purpose of degrading Him and making Him in very truth "the most abject of men." "For this death was not only the most painful but also the most shameful and infamous. Among the Jews, it was a malediction — to the Gentiles, abomination."[7]

What St. Chrysostom says is strictly in accordance with what we read in the classical authors of ancient Rome. Tacitus speaks of crucifixion as a death meet for slaves — "*Servile supplicium*" — and we know what, among the Romans, was the position of a slave. He was thought to be base and utterly vile; nay, less than that — "*Non tam vilis, quam nullus.*" Speaking of Asiaticus, who was an enfranchised slave, Tacitus says of him that "he expiated his abuse of power by the death reserved for slaves" — that is, crucifixion.[8]

In Juvenal, a native of Rome is made to say: "He is a slave, crucify him."[9] And Dionysius of Halicarnassus, in speaking of the suppression of a rising of slaves, also gives indirect evidence of this custom. "At once they were brought together, some from the houses, others from the public streets, and all were crucified."[10] Capitolinus tells us that Macro, for the sake of degrading the soldiers, put them to death by crucifixion, the punishment reserved for slaves.[11] The following passage from Cicero will serve to show the stigma of infamy, which was attached to this form of death. "It is a crime," he says, "to fetter a Roman citizen, an atrocity to scourge him, almost parricide to kill him. But what shall I say of putting him to death by crucifixion, which is of all torments the cruelest and most infamous? There is no word strong enough rightly to characterize such an abominable outrage."[12]

We find, in the life of the so-called divine Augustus — whose clemency is even yet spoken of by some — an incident which bears upon our point, while at the same time showing the value of the praise discerned by certain historians. I allude to what happened in Sicily after the civil war; how Octavius ordered a search to be made for the slaves, and those, whose masters could not be found to receive them back, he commanded should be crucified. Their number was about 6,000.[13]

Sometimes brave enemies were treated in the same way as slaves. During the siege of Jerusalem, Titus, surnamed the "delight of the human race," showed forth his kindness and generosity by crucifying daily some 500 Jews. This we have on the authority of Josephus, who adds that "there was not sufficient space for the crosses, nor crosses enough for each body, such was the multitude of those so put to death."[14]

Among the Romans no offence was considered more base or degrading than highway robbery. It reduced the offender to the level of a slave; and when caught, he was punished as such. Hence we find in their criminal code that brigands were to be crucified, and the execution to take place on the very scene of their crimes.[15]

The learned Père Laury, summing up the criminal legislation of the ancients, says: "Crucifixion was the death reserved for slaves, brigands, murderers, and rebels. They were suspended on the cross, and there left to die of pain, hunger, and thirst. After death they became food for dogs and crows. So that among the Romans this was at once the most infamous and the cruelest of punishments."[16]

The revolution Christianity has worked in men's minds is indeed fitly symbolized by the Cross. Until sanctified and transfigured by the death upon it of the Son of God, nothing was more repulsive or more shameful; thenceforth, no sign more glorious, more sacred, or more dearly loved. We, at this day, can hardly appreciate the miraculous power required to work such a change. We know the resistance it met with, and how it took three centuries of persecution and torrents of Christian blood to do away with the ancient prejudice. When, therefore, the Cross was finally exalted, appearing in the heavens, and afterwards publicly honored by the prince, who, in this sign, had won the empire of the world; we cannot be surprised at the rage and disgust shown by the proud patricians of Rome — and shown so openly, as to induce Constantine to transfer the seat of government. Strange mystery of the Providence of God, that this resistance to the power of the Cross should have furnished the very means by which its power was made most strong. One more example this, of what the apostle teaches: that "strength is made perfect in infirmity."[17]

Among the many ways of testifying their respect for the cross, the early Christian emperors used always to sign it on every decree, before writing their own name. Afterwards this came to be a general practice in signing documents of importance. The custom has survived, among the bishops of the Catholic Church, to the present day. Hence, also, those who cannot write still sign a cross, whenever they are called upon to witness the truth of any document. However ignorantly it may now be done, this was in its origin, and, in its nature, still is, a written act of Faith.[18]

To return from this digression, I must observe that crucifixion was not only employed as a means of punishment, but also as a terrible and salutary lesson for the multitudes. This lesson was a lasting one, for, except among the Jews, the bodies were always left hanging upon the cross until they either fell to pieces or were devoured by the birds and beasts of prey.

For this purpose of striking terror into the people, not only the baser sort of criminals, but also princes, were sometimes put to death in this manner by those who wished utterly to degrade them. Thucydides tells us of an Egyptian king, Inarus by name, who was treacherously taken and crucified by his own subjects.[19]

Justinus relates that, when Agathoclus was slain, several matrons were crucified by way of avenging the death of Eurydice.[20] The Carthaginians did not hesitate to crucify the most eminent citizens of their Republic. Thus they made examples of such generals as had contravened the orders of the Senate, even when by doing so they had won a victory.[21] We find something of the same spirit shown in the revolutions of modern times, as in the cases of Charles I and Louis XVI, and, more recently still, in that of the unfortunate Emperor, Maximilian of Mexico.

The torments of the cross were not only in use among the Jews, Carthaginians, and Romans, we find them also among the Greeks. According to Plutarch and Quintus Curtius, Alexander the Great was not less cruel sometimes than Augustus, Titus, and the others we have named.

Now it appears to us that we have said enough of the customs and criminal laws of the ancients to show that, both as a professional brigand and notorious malefactor, Dismas had necessarily incurred the penalty of crucifixion. He had, indeed, well deserved it, for he had grown old in wickedness. Having, according to the tradition, been a young man at the time of our Lord's flight into Egypt, he must, at the time of his death, have been about fifty or sixty years of age, some thirty or forty of which had been spent in robbing, pillaging, and murdering his fellow men.

Now at last the time had come for divine justice to put an end to his career. Through the instrument of human law many sins are punished, even in this world. And it is well that it should be so, for otherwise this earth would become a very slaughterhouse, where men would destroy each other like wild beasts.

True that many criminals escape altogether in this life, and that judgment is tardy, and that the just are astonished and confounded, continually crying out: "How long, O Lord, how long?" while the wicked, flourishing like the bay tree, reply: "There is no God!" But on the other hand there are many instances where the greatness of the punishment more than makes up for the delay in its infliction. This was the case with Dismas. Happily for him, justice proved to be but the forerunner of mercy.

Tradition does not tell us either the circumstances of his arrest or the spot where it took place. But it would appear that he and his companions were captured somewhere not far from

Jericho, in which town they were tried and condemned. Thence they were sent up to Jerusalem — probably by order of Pilate — that they might be executed in the capital at a time when the Paschal Feast should have brought together the largest concourse of people. This would have the double effect of making the usual spectacle of their sufferings, and of reassuring those who had so long been in fear and peril of their depredations.

In the meanwhile, it is hardly necessary to say that the two thieves must have been loaded with chains and immured in a dreadful prison. At Jerusalem the public prison joined on to the king's palace, which was close to the Prætorium. There it was that the criminals awaited the moment of execution.[22]

We do not lightly use the word dreadful in speaking of a Roman prison. These prisons consisted of subterraneous dungeons, damp, dark, and noisome, with no opening save an iron door, which never, even for a moment, admitted either light or wholesome air. In them the unhappy sufferers were confined with their feet in a sort of stocks, and an iron hoop round their necks, by which they were chained to the wall. The tortures they must thus have endured, were scarcely less bitter than death. To have a correct idea of the horrors of these places it is only necessary to visit the Mamertine prison at Rome.

I have been speaking of Roman prisons, because it was in one of such that Dismas awaited his end; but what I have said of them applies equally to those of all the pagan nations, whether ancient or modern. To this day the prisons in Turkey, in China, in the kingdom of Annam, in the empire of Morocco, in fact, in all the non-Christian States, are still a reproach and a disgrace. The law of love alone has softened the terrors of justice and mitigated the horrors of imprisonment, for it alone admits that, after condemnation, there is still room for repentance.

We do not know how long Dismas was left in prison, and we can only imagine, more or less approximately, what he was there made to suffer.

CHAPTER 5

The Scourging

B EFORE continuing the history of the sufferings of the Good Thief, it may not be uninteresting to some of our readers for us to give a few details about the Roman practice of scourging.

It is well known that the Roman magistrates, whenever they appeared in public, were always preceded by lictors carrying their fasces. These fasces consisted of rods of poplar, ash, and willow, or vine, about a yard long, bound up together, with an axe protruding at the top. They signified the two forms of punishment usually inflicted on criminals — i.e., scourging and beheading — which the lictors were always prepared to inflict on the spot. The dignity of a Roman magistrate, and his rank, might be ascertained by counting the number of lictors who walked before him; thus, a consul had 12 lictors, a prætor 6, and a dictator 24.

The lictors served exclusively as attendants upon the magistrates. Their duties were twofold — first, to walk before the magistrates with their fasces, opening for them a way among the crowds. This they did in single file. Secondly, they had to scourge the criminals. When the judge had pronounced his sentence, he added the command to the lictors that they should carry it out. Here are the words used: "*I, lictor, adde plagas reo, et in eum lege age.*" The lictors then seized the malefactor, bound and scourged him, and in certain cases put him to death. The name lictor comes from the verb *ligare,* to bind, as the first thing they did to the victim was to bind his hands and feet.

Scourging, however, was not always inflicted by means of the rods contained in the lictors' fasces. These were only one among five different instruments of torture. They were called by the Romans *virgæ,* and we find them preserved in the Russian knout, and the rattan of the Chinese.

Next there were the *loræ,* which consisted of strips of leather divided at the end, and sometimes weighted with lead.

Then there were the *flagra* and their diminutive, the *flagella,* whips made of several cords knotted at the ends. Varieties of this instrument were used by fathers in their families, masters in the schools, and also by the lictors when in court. Hence may be traced the practice of flagellation, which was in general use in France up to the end of the last century, and which was still retained in the navy until a very recent time. In the army and navy of England, it has not yet been abolished.[1]

The *fustes* were knobbed sticks or cudgels. They were called *scorpicnes* when the knobs were cut into sharp points, which tore and pierced the flesh of the victim. These were frequently used to torture the Christian martyrs.[2]

And finally there were the *nervi,* thongs of cow-hide, which, also, were generally weighted with lead.

These different instruments of torture were not all used at the same time. Choice was made among them, according to the condition of the person condemned and the sentence of the magistrate. The least degrading were the *virgæ,* or rods. These might be made use of to punish a free man,[3] but in no case was it permissible to scourge a Roman citizen; several laws, notably the Porcian and the Sempronian laws, expressly forbade it.[4] The extract from Cicero given above shows us what was thought of such a crime. Hence the terror of the magistrates of Philippi on discovering, as we read in the Acts, that the men whom they had scourged were Roman citizens. When the masters of the girl, having a pythonical spirit, apprehended Paul and

Silas, they had only to say they were innovators and Jews to procure their condemnation unheard. But, when the Apostles had been miraculously delivered from prison, and received permission to go their way in peace, Paul was indignant, saying: "They have beaten us publicly, uncondemned, men that are Romans, and have cast us into prison; and now do they thrust us out privately? Not so, but let them come, and let us out themselves." And when this was reported to the magistrates, they were sore afraid, and coming they besought them; and "bringing them out," says the sacred text, "they desired them to depart out of the city."(Acts 16:12-39)

The scourging here spoken of was the least ignominious, but that endured by our Divine Lord was the most shameful of all, and reserved for slaves, or those who, by their crimes, had forfeited all the rights of man. "He," as Baronius well remarks, "having taken upon Himself the form of a slave, also deigned to suffer the flagellation set apart for slaves."[5] In this depth of self-abasement, we may find the measure of His love.

Among the Romans the number of stripes was unlimited. It was left to be determined by the magistrate, and too often by the insatiable cruelty of the executioners themselves. Their ungovernable fury was such, that frequently they killed their victim, even when he was not condemned to death, but was only ordered to be scourged for some trifling offence.[6]

Not so, among the Jews. Their penal code was merciful, albeit severe, for it was inspired by Him, who is our Father, as well as Judge. We will quote the words of the text, for they show clearly the immense superiority even of the law of fear over the very best of merely human laws. "And, if they see that the offender be worthy of stripes they shall lay him down and shall cause him to be beaten before them. According to the measure of the sin, shall the measure, also, of the stripes be; yet, so that they exceed not the number of forty, lest thy brother depart shamefully torn from before thine eyes." (Deut 25:2-3) And the Jews were so careful not to transgress this merciful provision, that they always stopped short at the thirty-ninth stripe, as St. Paul bears witness: "Of the Jews five times did I receive forty stripes save one." (2 Cor 11:24)

Now, our Lord being condemned by Pilate, and not by the Jews, for whom it was no longer lawful to put any man to death, it follows that He must have been scourged according to the Roman method — that is, that He received an unlimited number of stripes.[7]

The two thieves were condemned by the same authority, and consequently must have been scourged in the same barbarous manner, though not probably to the same extent. It is also supposed that there was a further distinction made between them and our Savior, into which we shall enter at length in the following chapter.

CHAPTER 6

The Scourging *(continued)*

ACCORDING to the Roman usage, the scourging of a criminal took place either before he was led to execution, or on the way thither — "*Aut ante deductionem, aut in ipsa deductione.*" In the first case, it took place in the prison, or in the Prætorium, where judgment had just been given. After the sentence, as we have already seen, the judge added the command to the lictor, who immediately stripped the victim, tied his hands behind his back, and bound him hand and foot to a post or pillar. Then began the scourging, the horrors of which may be better imagined than described.

The same custom still prevails in the East, with this difference only, that the pillar is replaced by four stakes. How many times have our heroic missionaries undergone this fearful torment in China and Cochin China!

This practice of scourging in the Prætorium itself was the more ancient of the two; but, at the time of our Lord, it was not so usual as scourging on the way to execution.[1] Nevertheless, it was employed in regard to our Savior, as we read in the History of the Passion, (Mt 27:26; Mk 15:15; Jn 19:1) for what reason we cannot say.[2]

The pillar, to which He was bound, is religiously preserved at Rome, in the church of St. Praxedes. It is, as it were, a living, tangible monument, bearing powerful witness to the infinite love of the Son of God, and to the unspeakable heinousness of sin.

Nowhere do we find that the two thieves were scourged before going to Calvary. Now whereas the scourging formed a necessary part of the death penalty, it follows that it must have been inflicted on them on their way thither, which, as we have already said, was strictly in keeping with the usual practice in public executions.[3]

According to the ancient pagan writers, the torture was administered in this wise. First the criminal — generally a slave, whose guilt was not, perhaps, a tenth part that of his inhuman master — was stripped of all his clothes, next the cross was tied on his back, then the procession started, some of the executioners walking before the victim, dragging him with ropes, the others following behind with whips wherewith they scourged him without ceasing, until they arrived at the place of execution.

Here again we must pause to observe the perfect agreement of the Gospel with the teaching of history. The sacred text speaks of our Lord as going forth "bearing His own cross." (Jn 19:17) Plutarch tells us that "the criminal was always made to carry his own cross."[4] And Artemidorus says: "He first carries his cross, who is condemned to die upon it."[5]

Occasionally the Romans forced the unhappy slave's comrades to become the ministers of his death, and often they used to take delight in prolonging the torture by going the longest way to the place of execution. "An illustrious Roman," says Dionysius, of Halicarnassus, "having condemned one of his slaves to death, ordered his other slaves to execute the sentence. In order to make the punishment as public and notorious as possible, he commanded them to take him through the Forum and all the other most frequented thoroughfares, scourging him all the time, without ceasing. And thus they led him about the city, with the cross fastened to his outspread arms, and tightly bound across his breast and under his shoulders; those who followed striking and wounding, without pity, his naked body."[6]

Cicero and Livy make mention of the same sort of atrocity, without a word of pity or censure. The latter, describing the games, tells us that "all Rome being assembled in the circus, a certain father of a family commanded that one of his slaves should make the round of the arena, bearing his cross and being scourged, until the games should begin."[7]

Cicero speaks also of a "slave being scourged in the circus, while he was being led about carrying his cross."[8] It would appear that this cruel and degrading exhibition formed part of the pleasures of the Romans and one of their public sights. Arnobius tells us that it was one of their established customs;[9] a custom worthy indeed of the nation, foreseen by the prophet, under the figure of a beast with teeth of iron![10]

If therefore we wish to have an idea of the scourging of the two thieves, we must represent to ourselves that last, most ghastly procession, slowly wending its way towards Calvary.

First, we distinguish among the large crowds the trumpeters who precede the criminals, then comes a public crier, proclaiming their names and deeds, and finally the criminals themselves, one of whom is an old man. Both are stripped of their garments, and carry their crosses fastened to their backs, with their arms extended and bound to the two extremities. Both are dragged along by ropes, and followed by the executioners, who scourge them all the way from the Prætorium to Mount Calvary, a distance of thirteen hundred paces.[11]

Who knows but what this dreadful torture, undergone within sight of the uncomplaining Lamb of God, may have been for Dismas the beginning of a serious self-examination — the germ, indeed, of that repentance, which was to bear such glorious fruits on Calvary.

It will not be out of place to give here a few details as to those who were in all probability the means of executing upon our Divine Lord and the malefactors who died with Him the cruel torment of flagellation. These details appear to us to have a threefold interest — an historical interest, as shedding a light upon some usages of the ancients which are not generally known; a biographical interest, as showing us not only what the Good Thief suffered, but, also, at whose hands he suffered it; and, finally, a religious interest, as appertaining to the great Sacrifice of the Cross, every detail, in anyway connected with which, must always be welcome to the Christian mind. On this great subject our curiosity is more than legitimate; it is as noble as it is eager, and it would be hard indeed to satisfy its earnest craving.

The history of the Gabaonites is well known; how they deceived the people of God with their dry loaves, and torn, sewed-up bottles of wine, and worn-out clothes, and how, to punish them for their deceit, in pretending to come from afar off, Joshua condemned them, and their descendants after them, to become hewers of wood and carriers of water, in the service of all the people. (Joshua 9:22-27)

This setting apart of whole nations for certain menial offices was not unknown to pagan antiquity. We find examples of it at Sparta in the position occupied by the Helots, and, again, amongst the Romans. After the victories of Irebia and Trasimenus, when Hannibal tried to alienate from Rome the surrounding populations, the first to submit and attach themselves to the Carthaginian cause were the Picentii and Brutii. When, therefore, Hannibal had been driven out of Italy, these were the first also to feel the weight of the vengeance of Rome. Strabo tells us that "Picentia[12] was formerly the capital of the Picentii, but that now they dwell in the surrounding villages, having been expelled from their capital by the Romans in consequence of their having joined Hannibal, for which reason also they were excluded from military service, and condemned to be the messengers, foot-runners, and letter-carriers of the Republic."[13]

The punishment inflicted on the Brutii was more degrading still. They were condemned to serve as lictors to the magistrates of Rome. They were given at the same time many of the menial offices theretofore reserved for slaves; but of all these the duty of scourging was thought to be the most ignominious. To inflict this torture was considered almost as shameful as to suffer it.

In a very short time the name of Brutii came to be used indifferently with that of lictor. Thus, we find Cato, when accusing Quintus Thermus, reproaching him, among other things, with having had the decemvirs stripped of their clothes and scourged, because, forsooth, they had neglected to provide him with sufficiently good food! In his indictment, Cato speaks of the abominable outrage as having been perpetrated before all the people, who witnessed the decemvirs being scourged by the Brutii,[14] which term he makes use of instead of lictor, the two having become synonymous.

A certain number of this people were sent up to Rome at stated times, and distributed among the different magistrates, who took them with them into the various provinces.

Festus likens them to the Lorarii, or whippers, who in the old plays had to attend upon the magistrates, since the chief office of the Brutii was also to bind and scourge those condemned.[15]

Now, as the great commentator Baronius hesitates to affirm that the Brutii inflicted the torment of scourging upon our Divine Lord and the two thieves, it would be presumptuous in us to assert it in too positive a manner. We must observe, however, that for centuries their descendants, the Calabrians, were reproached with this crime, attributed to their fathers. The populace often preserve traditions, which have escaped the learned.

Thus much, at least, is certain, that about the time of our Lord, the Brutii still furnished the magisterial lictors; and that Pilate, as Roman Governor of Judea, must have been attended by them.

From Tertullian we learn that, later on, the soldiers, and others also, were sometimes called upon to scourge those condemned.[16] But whereas, in the History of the Sacred Passion, no mention is made of the soldiers having had anything to do with our Lord's scourging; we may reasonably conclude that the usual custom was not, therefore, departed from on that occasion, but that the Brutians were the ministers of His scourging, and, if of His, of the thieves' scourging also.[17]

CHAPTER 7

The Way of Sorrow

THE day and the hour of the crucifixion of our Lord and Savior, have been carefully handed down to us, both in the Holy Scriptures, and in the writings of the fathers. The time of our Lord's death, being that also of the death of the Good Thief, it is not, I think, straying beyond our subject, to enter into some detail concerning it. The day thereof fell upon a Friday, the 25th of the month of March, in the year of grace 33, the eighteenth of the reign of Tiberius Cæsar, under the consulate of the Gemini. And the hour, between the fifth and the sixth hour — that is, as we are about to show, between eleven and midday.

In the words of Tertullian: "The passion and death (of Christ) took place within the time of the seventy weeks, under Tiberius Cæsar and the Consuls Rubellius Geminus and Rufius Geminus, in the month of March, during the Paschal time, the eighth day of the Kalends of April, the first of the Azimes."[1]

St. Augustine speaks in the same sense: "No man denies that the Lord suffered on the sixth day before the Sabbath, for which reason this sixth day has been set aside for a fast."[2] "According to a tradition of the ancients, sanctioned by the authority of the Church, it would appear that He was conceived on the eighth of the Kalends of April, on which day also He suffered." Therefore Christ died upon the eighth of the Kalends of April; the two Gemini being Consuls."[2]

And St. Chrysostom: "Our Lord was crucified in the month of March, on the eighth of the Kalends of April, which is the paschal day of the passion of the Lord and of His conception. So that He was conceived on the same day as that on which He suffered."[3]

Summing up this ancient tradition (in favor of which it would be easy to cite many more witnesses), Venerable Bede speaks as follows: "Our Lord was crucified and buried on the sixth day of the week (Friday). . . . But that He was crucified on the eighth of the Kalends of April and rose again on the sixth of those Kalends is a commonly received opinion, well established by the consentient voice of an immense number of doctors of the Church."[4]

This date has been set down in the Roman Martyrology, and is so much respected that Roger Bacon at the end of the thirteenth, and Alphonsus Tostat in the fourteenth century, having ventured to impugn it, were both severely reprimanded by competent authority.[5] Some have opposed various astronomical tables to this venerable tradition. But in his *Régles sur l'Usage de la Critique*," the learned Honoré de Sainte-Marie has clearly shown that these tables contradict each other. Père Pétau also has proved them incorrect, after submitting them to a long and searching examination.[6]

Let us now consider the hour, at which the crucifixion took place. It is well known that the Jews did not observe the division of time now in use, but that they divided the day and night into four equal parts, each of their hours being equal to three of ours. The names of their day-hours have been religiously preserved by the Church, in memory of the several acts of the Sacred Passion. We find them in the Divine Office. The first is called *prime,* and this began at sunrise (Good Friday coming upon the equinox, it consequently began, on that day, at six o'clock); the second, *terce,* lasted from nine o'clock, till noon; the third, *sext,* from twelve, till three; and the fourth, *none,* from three, till six, in the evening.

At first sight, there would seem to be some difficulty in determining the precise hour of our Savior's crucifixion. St. Mark speaks of the third hour: "And it was the *third hour,* and they crucified Him." (Mk 15:25) Whereas St. John himself, an eye-witness, says: "And it was the parasceve of the pasch, *about the sixth hour,* and he saith to the Jews: 'Behold your King.' But they cried out: 'Away with Him, away with Him, crucify Him.' Pilate saith to them, 'Shall I crucify your king?' The chief priests answered: 'We have no king but Cæsar.' Then, therefore, he delivered Him to them to be crucified. And they took Jesus and led Him forth." (Jn 19:14-16)[7]

The contradiction between the two evangelists is rather apparent than real. We would follow the fathers of the Church, who hold with St. Mark that our Divine Lord and his fellow sufferers were fastened to the cross towards the *end of the third hour* — that is, a little before noon; and, with St. John, that they were lifted up about *the beginning of the sixth hour,* which would bring it to the same time of day. Or, as say the Apostolic Constitutions: "They fastened Him to the wood of the cross at the sixth hour; but, at the third hour it was, that they obtained the sentence of His condemnation."[8]

This death sentence, given during the third hour, was, so to speak, the crucifixion in germ, and the carrying out of the sentence during the end of that same hour and the beginning of the next, its practical development. "So that," as says St. Ignatius of Antioch, "by the permission of God, He received sentence at the hands of Pilate, on the Parasceve, at the third hour, and was crucified at the sixth hour."[9]

Now that we know the day and the hour of our Lord's condemnation, let us see what was the place, where sentence was passed upon Him, and upon the thieves. That place was the Prætorium, or house of Pilate. It had originally been the palace of the first Herod, and was situated at the foot of the rock on which was built the Antonian tower or stronghold. The remains of it are still to be seen, but the palace has been turned into a Turkish barrack. At a little distance from the chief block, was a smaller building, with a portico, in which the Roman guard were lodged. This was on the eastern side, facing towards Mount Calvary. Between it and the palace itself was an open court, paved with mosaic, according to the lordly custom of those times.

It was in this court, that the priests, and ancients, and all the people were gathered together, clamoring for the death of the Savior of mankind. As we read: "And they went not into the hall that they might not be defiled, but that they might eat the Pasch. And Pilate therefore went out to them."(Jn 18:28-29) Now the place, where Pilate came out to them, formed a sort of arcade in front of the halls of the palace, and here it was, that he spoke to them many times over, and strove to release their King; and here, that after the scourging, he said to them: "Behold, I bring Him forth unto you, that you may know that I find no cause in Him."

And "Jesus therefore came forth bearing the crown of thorns and the purple garment. And he saith to them: 'Behold the Man.'" (Jn 19:4-5) But they, far from being moved with pity, cried out the more: "Crucify Him, crucify Him."(Jn 19:6)

It may be some comfort to the Christian, to know that the arcade thus consecrated and made holy by the presence upon it of the Son of God, has lately been purchased by the community of religious entitled Daughters of Sion, and enclosed within a Church, where, day and night, these same children of Israel weep over and cry pardon for the sins of their fathers. God grant they may one day obtain also the conversion of their brethren!

The third hour was now far advanced, and every effort made by Pilate to save the Just Man had been foiled by the deadly hate of those, who through envy had delivered Him up. Seeing that they could not be brought to listen to the claims of justice, that they obstinately refused to admit His innocence, Pilate strove to set Him free on the score of mercy. He reminded them of their peculiar privilege. "But you have a custom that I should release one unto you at the Pasch. Will you, therefore, that I release unto you the King of the Jews?" (Jn 18:39) But this, also, proved vain. Then cried they all again, saying: "Not this Man, but Barabbas. Now Barabbas was a robber," (Ibid 40) one who had been guilty of murder and sedition.(Lk 23:19; Mk 15:7)

Let us reverently seek to pierce the veil and to understand the awful mystery hidden under this evil choice. The two men thus profanely brought into sacrilegious contrast represent the old Adam and the new — the old Adam, all steeped in crime; the new Adam, Christ, covered with wounds from head to foot; the old Adam, though justly condemned, set free and saved, by the new Adam undergoing the death penalty in his stead. This robber was a true type and symbol of the human race, degraded and vilified by robberies, and murders, and every species of sinful revolt against the laws of Nature and of God. In the King of the Jews, we find at once the Model and the Cause of our perfect regeneration. By His stripes we are healed, and saved through His life-giving death.

Sentence had been no sooner passed upon Christ than the prison-gates of Barabbas were flung open; by which was signified the breaking, by means of the Savior's death, of those heavy-wrought chains of sin which, during long thousands of years, had held man captive in the prison house of guilt. The barrier was at last thrown down, and the oppressed sons of Adam restored to freedom — even the freedom of the children of God.

Jesus, now being condemned to death, two malefactors were brought forth out of their dungeons to be executed together with Him. His enemies thought, by this means, to heap even greater shame upon Him, whereas they were but preparing the triumph of His mercy. Thus, in their blind fury, they were unconsciously working out the eternal designs of God, and marking the chosen Messias with yet one more of the signs foretold in prophecy. In the words of the Evangelist: "The Scripture was fulfilled, which saith: And with the wicked He was reputed."(Mk 15:28; Is 53:12)

Each of those condemned was made to bear his own cross. Our Savior was clothed again in His own garments, but the thieves went naked. The reason of this difference does not appear. It was necessary, however, to the fulfillment after his crucifixion of that other passage of Holy Writ: "They have parted my garments among them, and upon my vesture they have cast lots."(Ps 21:19; Mt 27:35; Mk 15:24; Lk 23:34; Jn 19:23-24)

Since morning the inhabitants of Jerusalem had been gradually flocking round the Prætorium. There was now a dense crowd, swayed to and fro by excitement and vicious hate. The state of frenzy to which their evil priests had worked them up was so fearful that it required the whole Roman cohort, numbering some twelve hundred men, to keep them within bounds. The signal at last was given for the death train to set out. This must have been towards half-past eleven, as the crucifixion took place about noon, and the distance between the Prætorium and Calvary is a little under a mile. The road thus traversed has been fitly termed the *Via Dolorosa* — the Way of Sorrow.

Our Lord, therefore, coming down what, in remembrance of Him, are now called the Holy Stairs, passed under that same arcade from the top of which He had been shown to the people.[10] Then crossing the outer court, He and his companions were led down the Street of the Palace, which, about two hundred paces beyond, was crossed by another street coming from the Gate of Damascus, anciently, the Gate of Ephraim. At the corner of this street, tradition tells us that Mary, the Mother of God, was standing, waiting to see her Son pass by. Coming out of this street was to be seen, so it is said, the house of the wicked rich man spoken of in the Gospel. The next street was straight, but very steep. About the middle of it, on the left, was the house of the holy woman, Veronica. Tradition has handed down to us the praise of her bold and glorious deed. Thus, we know how, being moved with pity and religious horror, she fearlessly made her way through the crowd, and came and reverently wiped with her veil the outraged, bleeding face of Christ. To reward her for this loving act of faith, He deigned to leave the print of His divine countenance stamped upon the linen.

Dismas, and the other thief, must have been witnesses of this, and they must, indeed, have marveled to see their fellow sufferer, at the same time, the object of such great love, and of hate so intense. Their wonder must have increased, when they saw a great multitude of women bewailing and lamenting Him; and still more at His sublime forgetfulness of self and shepherd-like care for the people when He, turning, exhorted them not to weep over Him, but for themselves and for their children. (Lk 23:27-31) These words, and the accompanying prophecy, must have sunk deep into the heart of the Good Thief; and, together with that divine prayer he was about to hear: "Father, forgive them, for they know not what they do," may very well be looked upon as the seed of that grace, which was soon to bear such glorious fruit on Calvary.

At the end of the street, in which Veronica's house was situated, was the Gate of Judgment, which those condemned had to pass through, on their way to the place of execution. In the time of our Lord, the city did not extend beyond. Even now, it is easy to trace the exact spot where the gate once stood.

In all the cities of Judea was to be found the Gate of Judgment. It was so called because the ancients of the people were wont to sit therein, administering justice. As we read in Deuteronomy: "If a man have a stubborn and unruly son, who will not hear the commandments of his father or mother, and being corrected, slighteth obedience, they shall take him and bring him to the ancients of his city, and to the Gate of Judgment, and shall say to them: 'This our son is rebellious and stubborn, he slighteth hearing our admonitions, he giveth himself to revelling and to debauchery and banquetings.' The people of the city shall stone him, and he shall die, that you may take away the evil out of the midst of you." (Deut 21:18)

Now, what was the reason for which the ancient Hebrews set down their tribunals in the very gates of their cities? Several reasons are given, of which the following are the two chief. The first, that all strangers, on coming to the city, should understand that justice was there meted out in true measure, and that all alike had equal right and opportunity for bringing forward their claims and wrongs. And thus all evil-doers would be overawed, or kept away by the sight of authority so firm and wakeful. Hence, among the Jews, the word *gate* was held to be of like meaning with that of *power.*

Of the word as used in this sense, we find the most solemn example in St. Matthew's Gospel. I allude to that sentence of our Divine Lord's which is to the Church, as it were, the charter of her immortality: "Thou art Peter; and upon this rock I will build my Church, and the *gates of hell* shall not prevail against it." (Mt 16:18)

This rendering of power by the term "gate" is still often met with in the East, notably in that phrase the *Sublime Porte,* which many pronounce without a thought of its original meaning. No wonder, however, that the meaning of the phrase should be forgotten, when the power signified thereby is gone.[11]

And, the second reason, why judgment was always given in the gate of the city, was that all discord and fighting should be kept without, the disputants not being allowed to enter the city until justice had been done and their feud made up. This necessarily tended greatly to the due maintenance of peace and order within the precincts.[12]

CHAPTER 8

Mount Calvary

BEYOND the Gate of Judgment is situated the hill of Calvary. But before touching its sacred soil, consecrated by such high and unspeakable mysteries, we will first attempt to give some description of the city of Jerusalem, which may serve as a help towards the right understanding of the Gospel narrative.

The city is built upon a mountain, the descent from which is abrupt and precipitous on every side, except on a portion of that looking westward. On the north it is bounded by the Valley of Jehoshaphat, on the east by that of Gideon, and on the south by that named Gehennah. The mountain is divided into several peaks or hills, of different heights, the most renowned of which is Calvary.

Let us listen for a moment to a venerable Eastern bishop, of the early Church, the illustrious master of disciples, yet more illustrious. I mean Diodorus of Tarsus, the teacher of St. Chrysostom, St. Basil, and St. Athanasius. He says: "Mount Moria was divided into several hills and peaks. The height looking eastward was called Mount Sion. This was the citadel of David. Close by was the threshing floor of Ornan, the Jebusite, which was bought by David and became the site of Solomon's temple, as we read (2 Paralip 3:1). Outside the walls of the city is that other height of Mount Moria, which is called Calvary, on which Isaac was sacrificed, and the Christ, Whom he prefigured."[1]

Later on we find other writers, not less reliable than the saintly Bishop of Tarsus, who divide Mount Moria into three principal hills — the first, Sion, so called by reason of its height; the second, Moria proper; the third, Calvary. On Mount Sion, the city and tower of David; on Moria, the Temple; on Mount Calvary, the Cross of Christ.[2]

The following is a further description of Mount Calvary, written a few years ago by Msgr. Mislin, whose learned work we have already had occasion to quote. "At the time of our Lord, Calvary was outside the walls of the city and beyond the Gate of Judgment. It was there that our Lord suffered, '*extra portam passus est*.' Today, however, the hill is within the circle of the walls. The reason of this is, that the present walls do not follow the line of the ancient ones.

"Recent excavations have brought to light what are undoubtedly the remains of the ancient walls. The best preserved part of them is near the Gate of Judgment. All the space beyond that, at present built over by the Church of the Holy Sepulcher, the Latin convent, and great part of the Greek convent, must have been outside the city. This portion of the present town was, at the time of our Lord, laid out in gardens, such as that of Joseph of Arimathea, and a few scattered houses, and was taken into the town by Agrippa the Ancient, about ten years after our Lord's death. These walls formed the third circumvallation of Jerusalem."[3]

In spite of this modification of the soil, Mount Calvary still bears sufficient proof of its identity in the marks indelibly impressed upon it at the time of the sacred Passion. Thus, in the same way, notwithstanding the changes the world has undergone, the earth holds always within its bosom the hidden fossil evidence of the truth of the Mosaic history.

The celebrated Adricomius, who, three centuries ago, examined the rent in the rock of Calvary, gives us the following description: "On the rocky mount of Calvary there still remains proof of the rending of the rocks. The rent is plainly discernible which was made at the moment of our Lord's death, to the right of this cross, just in front of the cross of the bad thief. Traces may yet be seen upon it of the Savior's blood. The opening is so wide as easily to admit the passage of a human body, and so deep is it that all attempts to sound it have been vain. It would seem as though it penetrated to the very center of the earth, so that as Christ's death opened to the Good Thief the way to Heaven, so the rending of the rocks opened for the bad thief, as aforetime to the rebel Cora, the road to hell."[4]

Let us now listen to the testimony of a later traveller, himself a Protestant, and cited by a great Protestant writer. "A highly estimable English gentleman once recounted to me how, in a journey which he had made throughout Palestine, he was accompanied by a very clever friend of his, a Deist, who, wherever they went, endeavored to turn into ridicule all that was told them by the Catholic priests concerning the holy places. In this irreverently satirical frame of mind this man went to see the rents of the rock, which are shown on Mount Calvary as the effect of the earthquake at the time of our Lord's death. The rock itself is now within the vast basilica built by Constantine.

"But when the Deist, who was also a naturalist, had made a careful examination and study of these openings, he said to his friend: 'I begin to be a Christian. I have long studied the physical sciences,' he continued, 'and I feel certain that the fissures in this rock cannot possibly be traced to any natural causes. An ordinary earthquake might have broken up the rock, it is true; but the cracks would have been made in a different sense. They would have followed the lay of the various veins or strata, and have been largest in those parts where the strata were narrowest and weakest. This is how we always find the breaks in such rocks as have been displaced and broken by means of earthquakes. But here it is far otherwise. The rock is transversely divided. The opening cuts straight through the strata in a most strange and inexplicable way. It seems, therefore, to me to be a clear proof of some supernatural and miraculous intervention; for which reason I thank God for having led me hither to contemplate this monument of His wondrous power — a monument which can leave no doubt of the divinity of Jesus Christ."[5]

As we have already said, Calvary is now within the walls of Jerusalem. The lower part of the hill is covered with houses; on the top of it is built the Church of the Holy Sepulcher. We have, as it were, examined the sacred rock itself; and now, before continuing our study of the tremendous mysteries there enacted, let us pause once more to explain the deep meaning of the name of Calvary.

The Syro-Chaldaic name of the mount is Golgotha, which may be rendered, "Place of the Skull." If we would know whence this strange designation, we must listen to the tradition of the venerable East. James Orrohaita (*sive Edessenus*) serves as its mouthpiece. He says: "When Noah entered into the ark, he took with him the bones of our first father, Adam. After the waters of the Deluge had subsided, and he came out again upon the dry land, the patriarch divided these precious remains among his three sons, giving the head to Sem, as being the eldest. To him also was given the land of Judea, when the brothers went forth to colonize the world. Whether of his own motion, or by order of his father, we know not, but certain it is that Sem buried the skull upon the hill which bears its name."[6] Thus was the first Adam laid where the Blood of the second Adam should be shed to wash away his stains, and give life to the world, in the very place where slept he, through whose disobedience death had entered into it.

However strange this tradition may appear at first sight, the most illustrious fathers of the Church, both in East and West, have not hesitated to accept and repeat it. We have already cited the venerable Master of St. Ephrem Syrus, and in our next chapter we shall give passages of the same import from many other fathers. Here, we would observe that the tradition is worthy of the wonderful ways of the Divine Wisdom, and, moreover, is in strict keeping with the natural feelings of man and the customs of the ancient patriarchs.

"All the people of the earth," says the learned Massio, "have always taken religious care of the remains of the illustrious dead. This feeling of respect is inborn in man, so that nowhere do we find that the bones or ashes of the dead have been treated as profane and worthless objects. Though separated from the soul, they have still within them, as it were, an indescribable germ of immortality, which shall, one day, re-clothe them in their flesh, and bud forth into life everlasting."[7]

In Egypt, as we know, the dead received even superstitious honors. Among the Romans, nothing was more sacred than the tomb, as is shown not only by their writings, but also by the number and magnificence of the sepulchral monuments they have left us. The same may be said not only of all civilized nations, but also of the savages themselves. We read of the aborigines of America that they retired before the invaders, carrying with them the bones of their forefathers. Why, therefore, should not Noah have done for his father — the father of the human race — what so many others, less religious than he, have done for their comparatively insignificant progenitors?

The care taken by his descendants of the bones of their ancestors is more than once recorded in Holy Scripture. When Jacob was dying, he desired his sons to bury his remains in the Promised Land, and they did as he had commanded them. (Gen 9:29; 1:13) And at the time of the Exodus, the Israelites did not neglect to take with them the bones of Joseph, according to the oath he had made them swear.[8]

There is no sentiment more natural or more healthy than respect for the dead, and low indeed must that nation be sunk, where their memory is neglected or their tombs left uncared for. Such neglect would show the basest ingratitude and corruption of heart, and, with a people so degraded, there would be little left to hope for.

CHAPTER 9

Mount Calvary *(continued)*

THE passages from the fathers, in which mention is made of the Calvarian tradition, are so numerous that it is impossible for us to quote them all. We shall, therefore, content ourselves with giving a few of the most striking.

We will begin with the testimony of the great apologist, Tertullian. "Golgotha," he says, "is the place of the skull; hence, sometimes, called Calvary. There the first man was buried, so we have been taught. There Christ suffered, and watered the ground with His Precious Blood, that, mixing with the dust of the old Adam, this Blood, together with the water out of the Savior's side, should cleanse it from all stain."[1]

The tradition which, in the second century, was taught in the Western Church, was not less widespread in the East. A great contemporary of Tertullian's speaks of it in these terms: "It is said that the place of Calvary was not unknown, but that rather it was in a special manner remarkable, and justly predestined to be the scene of the death of Him, Who died to save mankind. The tradition has come down to me that the body of the first man lies buried on the spot where Christ was crucified; that whereas in Adam all men had died, so in Christ all should live again. Thus on Calvary (the place of the skull) the head of the human race, with all his descendants, did rise to a new life, through the resurrection of the Savior, who there did suffer, and there did rise again."[2]

The great doctor of the Church, St. Basil, uses much the same language as that above quoted from Origen, but he adds several details respecting the father of mankind. "There is in the Church," he says, "a tradition which has been verbally handed down to us, according to which it would appear that the first inhabitant of Judea was Adam himself; that he established himself there, after being driven out of Paradise. Thus was this country, the first to receive the remains of a dead man, when Adam had paid the penalty of death. To that first generation of men, a head denuded of flesh was a strange and horrible sight. It made so strong and lasting an impression upon them that thenceforward they called the place, in which they had laid it, the Place of the Skull. It is improbable that Noah should have ignored the place, where the chief of mortal men was buried, and still more improbable that he should not have pointed it out to his children, after the Deluge. This being so, we may safely trace the tradition back to him. For this reason it was, that our Lord, having come to destroy death in its very root, elected to die on this said Place of the Skull, that, where death had taken its origin, there also life should begin its reign; so that death, which had prevailed over Adam, should from Christ receive its death blow."[3]

St. Epiphanius; who was a native of Palestine, and well versed in the traditions of his country, writes thus: "We have learnt from our most elementary books that our Lord Jesus Christ was crucified on Golgotha, the very spot where lay the body of Adam."[4]

And St. Athanasius: "Jesus Christ willed to be crucified on Mount Calvary, which, according to the belief of the most learned among the Jews, was the burial place of Adam."[5]

And St. Ambrose: "The spot on which was planted the cross of our Lord, was the very same place where Adam was buried. To this the Jews bear solemn witness."[6]

St. Chrysostom, commenting on the nineteenth chapter of St. John, makes mention of the same tradition.[7]

St. Augustine repeats it, together with that other tradition, which we have already given, in the words of Diodorus of Tarsus. He says: "Hear ye yet another mystery. The blessed priest, Jerome, writes that he has ascertained beyond doubt, from the ancients and princes of the Jews, that Isaac was offered up on the very spot where afterwards the Lord Jesus was crucified. . . . We also hear, from the tradition of the ancients, that the first man, Adam, was buried on exactly the same place where the cross was fixed, which place was called Calvary, from the head of the human race having been buried there."

"And in truth, my brethren, there is nothing unreasonable, in believing that the Physician was there lifted up, where lay the sick man; that where human pride had caused death, there the divine mercy should descend, and that the Precious Blood of Christ should wash, even in a physical sense, the dust of the first sinner, to redeem whose race, the Savior died."[8]

To this testimony we might add that of St. Cyprian, of Theophylactes, Metropolitan of Bulgaria, of Euthymius Zigolenus, of the Rabbi Moses Ber Cephas, of St. Germanus, Patriarch of Constantinople, of Anastasius Sinaiticus, and many others.[9]

Hundreds of years had passed since the early fathers had given their witness, but the tradition they had accepted and confirmed was still found living and fresh as ever when Adricomius and Quaresmus wrote the most learned of modern histories of the Holy Land.[10]

Quaresmus says: "It is believed that it was not only from a sentiment of filial piety, that the body of Adam was taken up and preserved in the ark from the destructive waters of the Deluge, but rather in consequence of a command which Adam had left to his descendants to bury him in the land of Juda."

"Among the mysteries which God had revealed to our first parent, the chief must have had reference to the Savior, Who was to come. It was made known to him that the Son of God would, one day, deign to die for us at Jerusalem, on the mount of Calvary. Nothing therefore was more likely, than that he should desire his children to bury his body on the spot, where Christ was to be put to death, that, participating in the fruits of that death, he might be called again to life there, where death had so long held him captive."[11]

It will be generally acknowledged, that a tradition which is authenticated by the almost unanimous testimony of the earliest and greatest fathers of the Church, and confirmed and reiterated by the most learned critics of modern times, may be well able to defy the attacks of the few who venture to impugn it.

Lest, however, they should quote in their favor the authority of St. Jerome, it is necessary, in the interests of historic truth, to sift thoroughly the opinion of that great doctor — the one exception to what we may call the *consensus patrum* on this subject. Before doing so, it may be well to remind our readers that it is a rule of evidence that one witness avails nothing as against a large number of other equally competent witnesses. Still less would the one dissentient voice be listened to, if it were found to be self-contradictory, or obviously mistaken. Far be it from me to speak in anything but the most respectful terms of the great solitary of Bethlehem, yet it is incumbent upon me to say that his testimony on the matter in question does fall within this class.

In his otherwise admirable commentary on St. Matthew, St. Jerome says: "I have heard it said that Calvary was the place where Adam was buried, and that its name is hence derived. For which reason, also, the Apostle says: 'Wake up, thou that sleepest, and rise from amongst the dead, and Christ shall be thy Light.' A pleasing interpretation this, and flattering to the ears of the people; but it is not true."[12]

Later on, however, the great doctor was less positive in repudiating this tradition. He mentions it in his commentary on the Epistle to the Ephesians, and then adds these words: "Whether these things be true or not, I leave to the judgment of the reader."[13]

And, later still, he affirms what he had at first denied, and afterwards given as doubtful. It is well known that the illustrious Roman matron, St. Paula, and her no less learned daughter, St. Eustochium, derived all their Biblical lore from the teaching of St. Jerome. We may, therefore, safely affirm that the following letter, written by them to their friend Marcella, was, if not, as some suppose, dictated, at least inspired by him: "It is said that in this city, on this very spot, Adam lived and died. Whence the place on which our Lord was crucified is called Calvary, as being the place where was buried the skull of the first man. So that the blood of the second Adam, in streaming from the cross, did wash away the stains of the first Adam and freed him from sin, and thus here fulfilled those words of the Apostle: "Wake up, thou that sleepest, and rise from amongst the dead, and Christ shall be thy light."[14]

I now think we have sufficiently shown that the evidence of St. Jerome is self-contradictory. It only remains for us to prove that he was mistaken in the first instance.

The reason St. Jerome gives for rejecting the Calvarian tradition is the seeming contradiction of it, to be found in the book of Joshua. Here is the passage in question: "The name of Hebron before was called Cariath-Arbe: Adam, the greatest among the Enacims, was laid there." (Jos 14:15) St. Jerome understood the Adam here mentioned to be Adam our first father. That this was his opinion is clearly proved by Baronius and Cornelius à Lapide. Whereas, Hebron was inhabited by the giant Arbe and his descendants, and hence the name of Cariath-Arbe — i.e., the City of Arbe. Now Arbe was the father of Enac, who was the father of the giants. And among the whole race, Arbe was still the greatest, whether by reason of his paternity, or by reason of his stature. For which cause he was also called Adam. That this is the true reading of the text can, we think, be easily proved.

First. It was in the valley of Hebron, anciently called Cariath-Arbe, that the giants lived in the time of Moses — those giants whose aspect so terrified the men he had sent to spy out the Promised Land. As we read in the text: "There we saw certain monsters of the sons of Enak, of the giant kind, in comparison of whom, we seemed like locusts." (Num 13:34)

Secondly. Josephus tells us that, in his day, it was still customary to show the bones of the giants, who had been buried on Hebron, and that they were of so huge a size as would appear incredible to any who had not themselves seen them.[15]

Thirdly. It is not possible to suppose that all the fathers above quoted should have passed over the said text of Joshua, and should have taught that Adam had been buried on Calvary, if this were contrary to Scripture. It is more reasonable to conclude that the Adam buried on Hebron was not Adam, the father of the human race.

Fourthly. That this is so, seems proved, moreover, by the very wording of the text. The Adam therein mentioned is termed great — "the greatest amongst the Enacims." Now, in connection with our first parent, the inspired writers never give any epithet whatever, so that such a phrase as this would be out of keeping with the whole tenor of Holy Writ.[16]

It is more reasonable, therefore, to believe that, in this instance, St. Jerome was laboring under a mistake which, later on, he himself corrected, as we have seen from St. Paula's letter to Marcella.

The tradition concerning Adam's having been buried on Calvary is still popularly shown forth in one of the most familiar of our symbols. I allude to the death's head so often to be found at the foot of the crucifix. For many of those who look upon it, the meaning is hidden, like that of such a number of the most instructive symbols. And yet how profoundly touching is its meaning! By this death's head at the foot of the figure of Christ, the connection is shown between the first and the second Adam; the sinner is placed under the expiator; death, sin's penalty, shows itself as vanquished by the death of the Just; and the whole human race is typified both as fallen in Adam, and as redeemed by Jesus Christ our Lord.[17]

There is yet another beautiful tradition attaching to the place of Calvary, of which we must say a few words, so that we may devoutly follow our Lord and His companions on their way thither, our minds deeply penetrated with all the types and figures, which shall prepare us fitly to enter upon the contemplation of this last, most tremendous mystery. This tradition tells us that it was on Calvary that was offered up the sacrifice of Abraham. The truth of it is most sure, for it rests on the double foundation of Scripture and the writings of the fathers. And the Lord saith to Him: "Take thine only begotten son Isaac, whom thou lovest, and go into the land of Vision, and there thou shalt offer him for an holocaust upon one of the mountains which I will show thee." (Gen 22:2) The land of Vision is, in Hebrew, the land of Moria — i.e., the land where is the Mount of Moria. We have already seen that Calvary is one of the heights of this mountain. When Abraham received the command to sacrifice his son he was living in the land of Gerara, whence to Mount Moria it was a three days' journey, as we read in Genesis: "on the third day, lifting up his eyes, he saw the place afar off." (Gen 22:4)

For patristic evidence we will content ourselves with citing St. Augustine, who gives us this tradition on the authority of St. Jerome: "Jerome the priest writes that he has learnt from the ancients of the Jews that it is beyond doubt that Isaac was sacrificed on the same spot where Adam was buried, and Christ crucified."[18]

This tradition is therefore true, beyond doubt. It is also singularly beautiful; full, indeed, of that ravishing beauty which is stamped upon every work of the Divine Wisdom. Let us observe the glorious relation, between the type and the antitype. By the order of his father, Isaac goes up the mountain, carrying the wood for the sacrifice. By the command, also, of His heavenly Father, Christ goes up the same mountain, bearing His own cross. Isaac, by his figurative sacrifice, marked out, fifteen hundred years beforehand, the sacred place where was to be accomplished the true and life-giving sacrifice of the Son of God. As the reward of their obedience Abraham and Isaac received those splendid promises, the best of which foretold the coming of Him in whom "all the nations of the earth" should "be blessed;" and He, the Promised One, received, as the price of His death, " all the peoples as His inheritance."

CHAPTER 10

The Crucifixion

BEFORE going up the mysterious Mount of Calvary, we think fit to pause awhile to inquire why it was chosen as the scene of our Lord's crucifixion. We have already said something of the reasons which had marked it out in the designs of the Providence of God; it remains for us to examine, what motives induced the enemies of Christ to become, themselves, the instruments for working out those designs.

The clue is easily found in a widespread custom of the ancients, preserved to us in history, which here again, as in so many other instances, confirms the truth of the Biblical story. The custom, I speak of, consisted in choosing the most frequented and most exposed places for the execution of criminals, so that the greatest possible number of persons might assist thereat, and learn from it what was thought to be a salutary and instructive lesson. Quintilian says, speaking on this subject: "Whenever criminals are put to death by crucifixion, we always select the most conspicuous among the places of public resort, so that as many as possible may see the execution, and be terrified thereby."[1]

This notion of the advantage of notoriety was not confined to the Romans, but was almost universal. Valerius Maximus gives us the following example of it among the Persians in their dealings with the Greeks. He is speaking of Polycrates, the famous tyrant of Samos. "This prince," he says, "became uneasy because of the uninterrupted success and happiness of his life; and so, fearing the jealousy of the gods, he sought to propitiate them by throwing into the sea, one of his greatest treasures, a very precious jewel. A few days afterwards, however, the stone was found again in the inside of a fish; and this was the end of his happiness. While Polycrates was meditating the conquest of Soina he was treacherously taken prisoner by Orœtes, the satrap of Cambyses, who caused him to be crucified on the highest peak of Mount Mycale, just in view of the town of Samos."[2]

For the sake of publicity a height was always chosen by preference, if one was to be found in the immediate neighborhood of the town where the criminal had been condemned. For the same reason the crosses were sometimes made extraordinarily high. Hence this cruel piece of irony, recorded by Suetonius in his life of the Emperor Galba: "One of those condemned to death loudly asserted his right as a Roman citizen and claimed the protection of the law. In derision Galba ordered that his cross should be made much higher than the others, so as to do him honor, and that, for further consolation, it should be painted white."[3] The exceptional height of his cross was to make him the more conspicuous, and its whiteness to mark him out as a Roman citizen, to whom alone belonged the privilege of wearing the white toga.

Let us return to the height of Calvary and witness the arrival there of Christ our Lord and His two companions. Some among the soldiery are digging the holes in which to plant the crosses, others seize their victims, and, throwing them down upon their backs, begin fastening them to the crosses they had carried thither. The huge crowd is looking on with various feelings, mostly hatred and cruel rage. Let us, also, approach, and, prostrate in spirit, wonderingly adore the innocent Lamb of God, the Victim of our salvation. What a mystery is here! In the words of St. Augustine: "There are here three crosses: on the one is the robber who is about to be made free; on the other, the robber who is about to be condemned; in the midst, Christ, the Savior of the one, the Judge of the other. How like the crosses! How immeasurably unlike, those who hang upon them!"[4]

As says St. Augustine, the crosses were alike; but what was that likeness? Among the ancients the form of the cross was not always the same. I think it not uninteresting to give some description of the five chief known varieties of this instrument, originally the most shameful of gallows, now become the most glorious of all signs.

First, we have the simple cross, the *crux simplex* of the Romans. This was merely an upright pole or broad stake, to which the victim was nailed in the same position, more or less, as on the other sorts of crosses. Often this form of cross was so low that the wild beasts could reach the person hanged upon it, and devour him while yet alive. Of this last horror we have two very famous examples. The one we find in Holy Writ, where mention is made of the crucifixion of the seven sons of Saul, given up by David into the hands of the Gabaonites. "And these seven died together in the first days of the harvest, when the barley began to be reaped. And Rizpah, the daughter of Aiah, took hair cloth and spread it under her upon the rock, from the beginning of the harvest till water dropped upon them out of Heaven, and suffered neither the birds to tear them by day, nor the beasts by night." (2 Kings 21:9-10)

The other example I spoke of is preserved to us by Eusebius in the celebrated letter of the churches of Vienne and Lyons. The passage treats of the death of the saintly Blandina, a martyr, and one of the glories of the latter illustrious church. "Blandina was then tied to a stake and given over to the wild beasts. At this sight, her companions were inspired with a new courage. They were filled with unearthly joy on seeing her nailed up almost in the same manner as Jesus Christ was nailed upon the Cross. They felt it to be a happy sign and a sure augury of triumph, for, under the appearance of their sister, it seemed to them as if they could discern Him, Who had been crucified for their sake. And thus they marched fearlessly to death in the sweet hope and belief that whosoever dies for the name of Jesus Christ, will receive new life in the bosom of the Living God."[5]

The second form of cross was called by the Romans *furca,* it being in the shape of a fork, having the same appearance as the letter **Y**. This was the sort of cross generally used for executing slaves. Apuleus speaks of it as being also used for other criminals. This, like the simple cross or stake, was so low as to allow the dogs and other animals devour the victim.[6]

Then we have the *crux decussata*, consisting of two pieces of wood placed cross-wise, the pieces being of equal length, and one end of each fixed in the ground. This cross may be represented by the letter **X**. It is popularly known as the cross of St. Andrew, it having been the instrument by which the martyrdom of that glorious apostle was finally accomplished, at Patras, in Achaia.

The fourth sort of cross was the *crux commissa*, a single pole with a cross bar over the top, in the form of the letter **T**.

And fifthly, the *crux immissa*, a straight piece of wood, with arms across the upper part. This is the cross which is most familiar to us, being used throughout the West, for which reason it is called, also, the Latin cross.

Now comes the question which of these various sorts of crosses served for our Lord and His two companions. The testimony of the fathers is divided on this subject. Tertullian, St. Jerome, and St. Paulinus, affirm positively that it was the *crux commissa.*

The first says: "The Greek letter *Tau*, which is also our T, is the figure of the cross."[7]

St. Jerome says: "In the ancient Hebrew alphabet, which is still in use among the Samaritans, the last letter, "*Tau*" (Tav) has the appearance of the cross."[8]

And St. Paulinus: "Christ triumphed over the powers of the enemy, not through the number or the strength of legions, but through the mysterious virtue of the cross, the figure of which, in the Greek letter **T**, expresses the number three hundred."[9]

The testimony of these fathers seems to us on this point to be preferable to that of some others equally venerable — such, for instance, as St. Justinus, St. Irenæus, and St. Augustine, who seem to incline rather towards the ordinary Latin form.

Our chief reason for adopting the former opinion is this. Our Lord throughout his life, and especially in the smallest details of his Sacred Passion, fulfilled every type and every prophecy. Whence in very truth he was able to say, when expiring upon the cross, "It is finished."

Now, the *crux commissa*, of which we are speaking, furnishes us with the antitype of two great figures of the Old Testament. In the passages above cited, Tertullian and St. Jerome both refer to this text of Ezechiel: "And the Lord said to him, 'Go through the midst of the city, through the midst of Jerusalem, and mark *Tau* upon the foreheads of the men that sigh and mourn for all the abominations that are committed in the midst thereof.'" And the further command to the destroyers: "But upon whomsoever ye shall see *Tau*, kill him not." (Ez 9:4) That *Tau* was at the same time, the material form and the mystical figure of the cross. Signed on the foreheads of the just men of Jerusalem, it saved them aforetime from temporal death, as we read in the vision; signed upon the foreheads of the followers of Christ, it shall save them from that worse death, which is to everlasting.

There is yet another mystery connected with this form of cross. According to the Greek system of numeration, the letter Tau has the value of three hundred. Now, it was with this mystical number of three hundred men that Gideon overcame the Madianites. In the figure, Gideon goes down into the camp by night. His soldiers each carry a lamp, hidden within an earthen pitcher. At a given moment, the pitchers are broken and the light of the lamps suddenly shines forth, the trumpets blow, and the enemy are so panic-stricken that they all take to flight. Let us now look at the reality, foreshadowed by the sword of the Lord and of Gideon.

Amid the darkness of Calvary, the humanity of Christ, under which the God-head lay hidden, is torn and broken by the agony of the cross. The light of His divinity shines forth in great signs and wonders, and with the *Tau* — the mystical three hundred — the true Gideon puts to flight the powers of hell.

The tradition concerning the true form of the cross may still be found in the Missal, where, at the beginning of the Canon of the Mass, there is always a representation of the Crucifixion. This picture, or engraving, which we see in the modern editions, was confined in the ancient missals to a small cross painted under or within the T, commencing the words, "*Te igitur, clementissime Pater*;" so that at the beginning of this most sacred part of the mass the figure and the reality, the type and the antitype, were brought together, and, so to speak, confounded in one. This small detail of symbolism is known to very few, although pointed out by the learned Pamelius so many hundred years ago.[10]

Nevertheless, as we have already said, some of the fathers describe the cross in the way in which we generally represent it. How can we explain their mistake? The difficulty is solved for us by Innocent III, who, speaking at the fourth Council of the Lateran, says: "The *tau* is the last letter of the Hebrew alphabet. It expresses the form of the cross, such as it was before Pilate caused it to be surmounted by the title of our crucified Lord."[11]

The historian Nicephorus is equally explicit. Speaking of the finding of the Holy Cross by St. Helena, he says: "Three crosses were found near together, and the white tablet on which Pilate had written 'King of the Jews,' in several languages — which tablet had been fixed above the head of Christ, in the form of a column, so that the crucified One should be known to be the King of the Jews."[12] And, finally, the Gloss says, in so many words: "The tablet (or placard) placed above the cross formed, as it were, a fourth arm."[13]

"This being so," says Sandini, "it is easy to reconcile the apparent contradiction. Those fathers who speak of the Cross of Christ as being in the form of the letter T — that is, a *crux commissa* — describe it without the tablet bearing our Lord's cause or title; and those who call it a *crux immissa*, having four arms or extremities, speak of it in conjunction with the tablet, which was placed upon it."[14]

We do not think it necessary to apologize for the length of our digression, for who could find wearisome details which help us to know the Cross of Christ, such as the world saw it, once, and shook to its very center; such as it will see it again, when, the end being come, the heavens and the earth shall, with a great noise, pass away? In the Cross is the mystery of mysteries. It is the trophy of the Son of God, the blessed instrument of our Redemption; in a word, our joy and comfort in this life, and our hope in the latter day, when, to the great terror of the wicked, it shall appear in the heavens telling forth the second coming of Christ: when He shall judge the world, and, in the face of the assembled peoples, render to every man according to his works.

CHAPTER 11

The Suffering of the Cross

WE come now to the crucifixion itself. It would be a mistake to suppose that the two thieves were fastened to their crosses by ropes instead of nails, as we sometimes see them represented. All, who were crucified, were invariably nailed to the cross. So universal was this custom that, in the words of an ancient writer: "The cross was made up of two things; the wood and the nails."[1]

St. Augustine, who was so thoroughly acquainted with all the usages and customs of antiquity, speaking of those crucified, says: "They continued to suffer long after the nails had been hammered through their hands and feet." And, speaking of the Good Thief, he says: "his body was transfixed by the nails, but not so, his soul. Nor was his mind enfeebled."[2]

And St. Chrysostom gives the same testimony: "Who can fail to admire (the Good Thief), who, though transfixed with nails, yet preserved his mind and sense untroubled."[3]

Tradition is unanimous on this point. We refrain from quoting all those who have made themselves its organs, lest in doing so we should over pass our due limits.[4] Suffice it to say that the evidence is so conclusive that we may affirm, with the learned Gretzer, that "it is not possible to understand how crucifixion could be inflicted without nails."[5]

Now comes the question, What number of nails were used upon Calvary? The number was the same for our Lord and for the two thieves. Now we learn from tradition that our Lord was fastened to the cross with four nails — two nails through His hands, and two through His sacred feet. Lucas Tudensis, surnamed the Solomon of Spain, cites, and comments as follows, the testimony of Innocent III on the subject: "That four nails were fixed in the body of the Lord is proved by the witness of that great vicar of Christ, doctor of the Church, and implacable foe of heresy, Innocent III, who speaks in these terms: 'In the Passion of the Lord there were four nails, which served to fasten his hands and feet to the cross.' What can be clearer than this saying? What more true than these words which come from the throne of God — that is, from the Roman Church, by the mouth of our common Father, Innocent."[6]

To represent our Lord, or the thieves, fastened to the cross with only three nails, is therefore at variance with the ancient tradition. I may add that it is contrary to reason. For how could one nail be made to go through and hold two feet placed one over the other? The operation would be, if not impossible, at least most difficult, whereas with two nails nothing could be easier. These nails were of a square shape, about five inches long, of a proportionate thickness, with great round heads. It would be hard to imagine anything more dreadful than the agony inflicted by nailing through the hands and feet. One cannot bear to think of, much less to describe, the horrible consequent rending and tearing of the nerves and muscles and delicate fibrous tissues of the flesh.

In speaking of the nails we must not omit to mention the *suppedaneum,* which, together with them, served to hold the body fixed upon the cross. This *suppedaneum* was a piece of wood fastened to the lower part of the cross, and which served as a sort of rest for the feet, not sufficient, indeed, perceptibly to diminish the suffering involved in the hanging position of the body, but still giving enough support to prevent the hands being torn in two through the excessive tension momentarily enlarging the wounds of the nails. In this manner the danger was obviated, which otherwise would have been very real, of the victim falling off the cross. By the later Latin writers the *suppedaneum* was also sometimes called *sedile* and *solistaticulum*. Innocent III speaks of it in these terms: "There were, in the cross of the Lord, four pieces of wood — the standing-up post (or tree); the cross-bar; the stem (or rest), placed beneath (the body); and the title, placed above."[7]

Once fixed upon this bed of pain, the victims were lifted up so that all the people might enjoy the sight of their torments. The cross, in falling into the hole prepared for it, must have given their whole system such a shock as is frightful to think of. In fixing it with wedges and sods, pounded and hammered roughly together, this torture must have been some time continued, and even increased.

What was the height of the cross? As we have already seen, the height often varied according to the rank of the criminal. But in our Lord's case no distinction seems to have been made between Him and the two thieves. St. Augustine tells us that the three crosses were alike, which later on was proved, at the time of the finding of the cross, when nothing short of a miracle was required, to show which had been sanctified by the Savior's death and Blood.

An ancient and venerable tradition affirms that our Savior's Cross was fifteen feet high, and that the arms, or cross-bar, were eight feet from end to end.[8] These dimensions, though large, do not seem to be anywise exaggerated.[9] If we suppose, as is most probable, that the crosses were sunk about a foot-and-a-half into the ground, the head of our Lord, and consequently also those of His companions, must have been about thirteen-and-a-half feet from the ground. That the cross was of some considerable height seems proved by the Gospel record, since it was necessary for the man, who gave our Lord vinegar to drink to put the sponge containing it upon a reed, so as to reach His sacred Mouth. (Mt 27:48; Mk 16:36) Whether from the intensity of their blind fury, or out of deference to the Jews, or from fear lest some miraculous intervention should deprive them of their victim, or whether, perhaps, merely in order to make their King appear the most guilty of the three men condemned — certain it is that our Lord was crucified the first, and upon the highest peak of Calvary, the other two crosses being planted on each side of Him, on the slope of the hill. It would appear that, having crucified the Lord of Glory, the bloodthirsty rage of the soldiers and surrounding Jews was almost satisfied, and that they proceeded but slowly with the two other executions. The words of St. Matthew and St. Mark seem to warrant this opinion, which is nowise contradicted by the other two Evangelists. St. Matthew says: "And after they had crucified Him, they divided His garments, casting lots. . . . And they sat and watched Him. And they put over His head His cause, written — 'This is Jesus, the King of the Jews.' Then were crucified with Him two thieves, one on the right hand and one on the left." (Mt 27: 35-38) And St. Mark: "And crucifying Him, they divided His garments, casting lots upon them what every man should take. And it was the third hour, and they crucified Him. And the inscription of His cause was written over, 'The King of the Jews.' And with Him they crucify two thieves; the one on His right hand, the other on His left." (Mk 15:24-27) It would also seem probable that the two thieves each had their cross surmounted by a tablet, showing forth the cause of their condemnation.[10]

Be this as it may, there can be no doubt that the thieves, like our Lord, were crucified naked. Such was the invariable custom of antiquity. We find confirmatory proof of the custom in Artemidorus, who gives us the following revolting jest: "Crucifixion is a benefit for a poor man, for he is thereby exalted; but for the rich man it is an evil, because he is crucified naked."[11]

Of the terrible suffering endured upon the cross it is difficult, nay, impossible, to give any adequate idea. St. Augustine says: "Among all the forms of death there is none worse than this. Wherefore when our pains become most intensely cruel we speak of them as being *excruciating*, which now is derived from *crux* (the cross). Hanging suspended on the tree, their hands and feet pierced through with nails, those crucified died a slow and lingering death. To crucify was not to kill. [The victim] lived on some time upon the cross, not because the executioner meant to prolong life, but rather to protract death, that so the agony should not too soon be over."[12]

And yet, one would almost think the suffering was too intense to last. On the cross, every portion of the body underwent the most fearful torture. Hanging in this manner suspended upon four nails, it was impossible for any part to be rested, or even for one moment eased, from the terrific strain. The nerves were contracted in violent spasms, and the whole frame was convulsed with agony. The body becoming more enfeebled every minute through loss of blood, each member became momentarily more sensible of pain. To all these torments must be added that of a devouring thirst. To be in this state for hours, having no hope but death, and feeling that to be still afar off, to be loaded with the jeers and reproaches and insults of the multitudes, without a single word or look of compassion, without having within him a single consolatory thought, was indeed more than human strength could bear. Can we wonder that the parched, fevered lips of the bad thief should have uttered blasphemies that he should have given himself up to despair?

Blinded with suffering and shame, Dismas and his companion strove to vent their rage upon their fellow sufferer. His calm, unruffled patience and His silence formed such a strange contrast to their convulsive cries and rage! They had heard it said that He was the Son of God; on His cause, it was written that He was the King of the Jews. At the foot of His cross, they saw a small, but faithful, band of devoted friends. The multitudes, indeed, mocked and blasphemed Him; yet many among the crowd were weeping over His sufferings. If He were in truth the Son of God, why did He not stretch forth His hand to save Himself, and them? "If Thou be the Christ, save Thyself and us!" (Lk 23:39) The entreaty was uttered with scorn and rage; not, alas! in faith. They did not, could not, believe in a God so outraged, so smitten, so despised. Yet salvation was close at hand. But their hearts were too hardened, and it needed a miracle to change and enlighten them. And so they also reviled the Lord, (Mk 15:32) and repeated the taunts and blasphemies of the priests and ancients of the people. (Mt 27:44)

But, now is it true, that both the robbers blasphemed against the Lord? St. Luke speaks only of one: "And one of the robbers who were hanged blasphemed Him, saying, 'If Thou be Christ, save Thyself and us.' But the other answering, rebuked him." Upon the authority of this text, several of the fathers have tried to prove that the bad thief alone blasphemed. The greater number, however, are of a contrary opinion. They quote in proof the words of St. Mark: "And they that were crucified with Him reviled Him,"[13] and of St. Matthew: "And the selfsame thing the thieves also, that were crucified with Him, reproached Him with."[14] The learned commentator, Cardinal Hugo, solves the difficulty by explaining the apparent contradiction. "We had rather, and better, say, that in the beginning (Dismas) blasphemed with the other robber, but that Christ our Lord having visited him by His merciful grace, he then repented." (Mt 27)

We find the same interpretation given by Titus, Bishop of Bosra, who wrote in the fourth century. 'What is the reason," he asks, "that St. Matthew and St. Mark affirm that both the thieves reviled Christ, whereas St. Luke only accuses one (of them of this crime)? At first both the thieves blasphemed Him, like the Jews. Maybe they hoped thus to buy their favor, and obtain pardon, or at least some alleviation of their sufferings. But afterwards, being disappointed of the benefit they had looked for, one of the thieves repented, and earnestly exhorted his companion to examine (his past life and acknowledge the justice of his sentence.)"[15]

If therefore, as seems most probable, the Good Thief did blaspheme our Lord, his conversion is all the more striking, and yet more worthy of admiration. We will now endeavor to recount it. It will be as balm to the soul after all the harrowing details we have so long dwelt upon, in this and the preceding chapters.

CHAPTER 12

Conversion of the Good Thief

S
UCH was, towards the hour of noon, the aspect of Calvary on the great day of our Redemption. On the highest point of the mount was planted the cross of the Son of God; a little lower down, on the slope of the hill, the cross of Dismas on the right hand and that of the bad thief on the left. Round about the three crosses was an open space surrounded and guarded by the Roman troops. At the foot of each cross, a small band of soldiers, who sat and watched. Near them were Mary, the Mother of Jesus, and John, the beloved disciple, and those other women whose mysterious privilege it was to stand by the Cross of Christ. Beyond the open space, a countless multitude were continually coming and going, succeeding each other like the waves of the sea, and all, save the chosen few, blaspheming and reviling the Lord, as they passed by.

Here all is mystery — mystery of suffering, mystery of self-abasement, mystery of insult and shame, mystery also of ingratitude, and, above all, mystery of love! In all these mysteries, the true, perfect, and literal fulfillment of the prophets. Let us strive to enter into yet another mystery, which, although of less moment, is yet full of comfort and instruction. I mean the mysterious significance of the position chosen for the Cross of our Lord, placed as it was between, or in the midst of, the two thieves. Thereby is signified His character of Mediator possessed by none other but

Him. For He is our sole Mediator, in Heaven or on earth; during His mortal life, as at the hour of His death; now, henceforth, and for evermore.

"The place of a mediator," says St. Ephrem, "is a middle place, between, or in the midst. It is from between the two criminals of Calvary, that Jesus makes Himself known as the universal Mediator. Always and everywhere, His place is in the midst. In Heaven, He holds the middle place, between the Father and the Holy Spirit. On earth He is born in a stable, in the midst of angels and men. He is placed as the corner stone, in the midst of the peoples. In the ancient covenant, He is in the midst of the law and the prophets, whose Lord, He is. In the new covenant, we see Him on Mount Tabor, with Moses and Elias, He Himself in the midst. On Calvary, He shows Himself again, but in the midst of two thieves; and to the Good Thief He reveals His Godhead. He is the Eternal Judge, placed between this present and the future life, between the quick and the dead; source alike of the life we now enjoy, which is for a time, and of that never-ending life, which is to everlasting."[1]

And what does Christ do, in this midst? "He does two things," replies St. Cyril; "He confounds the wicked and protects the good. He does, for all time, and among all nations, what the pillar of the cloud did in the wilderness, when it prevented the two camps from joining in fight; showing itself as a dark cloud to the Egyptians and hindering their advance, but as a pillar of fire to the Israelites, enlightening the night. Divine Providence had so willed that, on Calvary, Christ should be in the midst of the robbers, of whom one is converted and saved; the other repents not and is condemned. The type and figure, these, of the elect and the lost."[2]

Now, it is matter of faith, that at the last day the just will be on the right of the Sovereign Judge, and the unjust on His left. "And all nations shall be gathered together before Him, and He shall separate them one from another, as the shepherd separateth the sheep from the goats: and He shall set the sheep on His right hand, but the goats on His left." (Mt 25:32-33)

So that nothing might be wanting to complete the likeness of the Calvarian type, the Good Thief was therefore placed on the right of our Lord, and the bad thief on His left. True, that there is no mention of their relative positions to be found in the Gospel, but this, like many other precious details, has been preserved to us by tradition. The fathers give a unanimous witness to its truth. We will content ourselves with quoting St. Augustine and St. Leo.

St. Augustine says: "Note well, and you will see that the Cross, itself, became a judgment-seat. In the midst, is the Judge; on the one side, the robber who believes and is set free; on the other, the robber who blasphemes and is condemned. Already (the Lord) showed forth what He will do with the living and the dead, who shall likewise be placed, some on the right hand and some on the left. The Good Thief is the figure of those, who shall be on the right hand; the bad thief of those on the left. Judged Himself (the Son of Man) threatens judgment."[3]

And, later on, St. Leo, the Vicar of Him crucified, tells us: "Jesus Christ, the Son of God, is fastened to the Cross which He had Himself borne, and with Him likewise are crucified two thieves, one on His right hand and the other on His left; so that, even on this gibbet, that should be, in some sort shown forth, which is to take place at the final judgment; (I mean) the separation (of the just from the unjust). The faith of the believing robber, is the figure of those saved; and the wickedness of the blasphemer, the type of those condemned."[4]

Long had the Savior hung upon the cross, amid the most fearful agony of body and soul. To the insults and derision and blasphemous mockeries of the Jews, and their princes and priests, He had hitherto opposed a sublime and unbroken silence. But now fearing, as it were, lest the divine vengeance should overtake their crime, He cries aloud for mercy towards those who had shown Him none: "Father, forgive them, for they know not what they do!"

Scarce had these life-giving words been uttered, when Dismas ceased to blaspheme. All the crowd had heard them, but he at least had understood their meaning, and he, on the instant, sought and obtained their fruit. He was not content with repenting himself, but turning, he exhorted his companion to do likewise. "And he rebuked him, saying: Neither dost thou fear God, seeing thou art under the same condemnation? And we, indeed, justly, for we receive the due reward of our deeds, but this man hath done no evil." (Lk 23:40-41)

This is indeed a wonderful change, that he, who, a moment before, was blaspheming and reviling, should now rebuke his companion for doing the selfsame thing. Where, Dismas, shall we find a clue to the mystery? What miracle has converted thee? Who has revealed to thee the innocence and the dignity of thy fellow sufferer? The Lord is not come down from the cross, yet now, in truth, thou believest that He is the Son of God? Thou hailest as King, Him Who is dying upon the tree of shame. And He, the reproach, the outcast of the people — Who, stripped and naked and covered with wounds, had become, as it were, a worm and no man — He replies to thy homage by promising thee a place in His kingdom: "And he said to Jesus: 'Lord, remember me when Thou shalt come into thy Kingdom.' And Jesus said to him, 'Amen, I say to thee this day thou shalt be with Me in Paradise." (Lk 23:42-43)

Full of wonder and admiration, St. Leo asks again: "Whence has (Dismas) received his faith? Who has explained the mysterious doctrine? What preacher has inflamed him (with love)? For he now confesses, as his Lord and King, One who (outwardly) seems to be no more than his fellow sufferer?"[5]

Ah! with rare instinct the Good Thief had, as it were, penetrated the disguise and recognized the features of his companion. He now strives to seize upon His riches, as he had so often, in his past life, plundered the goods of those who came in his way. "Even on the cross," says St. Chrysostom, "he did not forget his former cunning, but secured as his booty the kingdom (of heaven)."[6] And, with one voice, all the fathers praise him for this new act of spoliation. "This happy robber," says St. Ambrose, "meeting the Lord on his journey, strives to possess himself of His treasure, according to his usual practice."[7]

St. Augustine breaks forth into rapturous praise of our saint: "Blessed is this thief; yea, I say, blessed, in that he no longer spreads his snares alongside the road, but takes hold of Christ, who is Himself the way, from whom also he obtains life by a new sort of robbery, and through death he is confirmed in everlasting possession of his spoils."[8]

Let us not lose a similar echo from one of our great Christian poets, whose voices, unhappily, are heard by so few. In a song overflowing with the noblest enthusiasm, Sedulius says of the Good Thief that "he seized, as plunder, even the kingdom of Heaven."[9] Thus the brigand's nature remains the same, although so marvelously changed! But how did Dismas recognize his kingly fellow traveler? Whence did he obtain knowledge of His treasures? From whom did he learn this new and unfailing mode of attack? Let us entreat of the Divine Victim, grace, in order to the right understanding of the mystery. If we ask with an earnest, humble spirit, He, our Savior, will not fail to show us these first-fruits of His redemption.

CHAPTER 13

Causes of the Good Thief's Conversion

"And I, if I be lifted up from the earth will draw all things to Myself." (Jn 12:32).

THUS spoke the Savior, and His words are very truth. We see the beginning of their fulfillment while yet He was still hanging upon the Cross. Dismas was the first of those so drawn. It will not be a fruitless endeavor, for us to search out and examine what were the means employed for his conversion. In every conversion there are always two things to be considered — the active or inward cause, and the instrumental or outward cause. The active cause is that which directly produces conversion. The instrumental cause is the means employed by God for making the active cause to enter into the soul.

This being so, it follows that the active cause of the conversion of the Good Thief, like that of all sinners, in every age and station, was none other than divine grace. What is grace? Who shall be able worthily to define it? It is a free gift, an undeserved bounty, a light for the darkness of our spirit, a something which touches and changes the heart with exquisite charm and irresistible power; in a word, it is a divine influence, which, doing away with the perverse and corrupt inclinations of the old man, puts in their stead the noble thoughts and longings of the new — destroys the bad leaven, and forms him it acts upon into a new paste, so that, from sinner that he was, he becomes a penitent, a just man, and a saint. Such is grace, so far as my weak words can paint it.

Grace has its unfailing source in the infinite mercy of God. Therein we find the clue to every conversion. Long ago, God revealed their secret by the mouth of his prophet, saying: "I have loved thee with an everlasting love, therefore have I drawn thee, taking pity on thee."(Jer 31:3). Hence, if we ask of Dismas the cause of his conversion, he will reply, in the words of St. Paul: "By the grace of God I am what I am;" and, verily, he might add: "and His grace in me hath not been void."(1 Cor 15:10)

St. Cyril of Jerusalem, analyzing, as it were, the soul of Dismas, speaks of his conversion in these terms: "What power has enlightened thee, O thief? Who has taught thee to worship one despised, and, like thee, nailed to the cross? O Eternal Light, that shinest on those in darkness! It is then just, O thief, that thou shouldst hear the words: have confidence; not that thou hast cause for trusting, in thy works, but because the King is beside thee, Who giveth grace."[1]

And St. Gregory the Great, speaking of the wonderful change so worked, says: "He ascends the cross as a most notorious malefactor, see what he is become through grace! He rejects not grace, and suddenly he is filled therewith and is faithful to it even unto death."[2]

The great commentator, Cornelius à Lapide, asking the cause of our saint's conversion, makes answer in these words: "He was inwardly touched by a rare and almost miraculous grace of God, which, enlightening his soul, revealed to him the innocence of Christ, His kingly rank, and the sovereign power by which He was able to raise the dead; so that (Dismas) was moved to recognize in Him the Messias, the Son of God and the redeemer of the world."[3]

As to the active cause of the Good Thief's conversion, there can, therefore, necessarily be no doubt whatever; but, as regards its instrumental cause, there is considerable difference of opinion. In the Gospel, we find mention of several sudden and even instantaneous conversions, but in each case the instrumental cause of conversion is clearly pointed out. Let us take that of St. Matthew, the publican Levi, whom our Lord found sitting at the receipt of custom. "What is (this) receipt of custom?" says St. Chrysostom. "It is an iniquity sanctioned by law . . . A publican is harder than thieves. . . . (For) what is the receipt of custom? A shameless sin, worse than highway robbery, not having the same excuse. A thief, while he is stealing, may at least feel ashamed; whereas a publican robs without remorse."

Zaccheus also was a publican, possibly even more dishonest than Levi. He, likewise, in the twinkling of an eye, became a model of penitence and holiness. But in his case again we have the instrumental cause of conversion put before us in those words of our Lord: "Zaccheus, make haste and come down, for this day I must abide in thy house." (Lk 19:5) Salvation came unto this son of Abraham, while yet he was up in the sycamore tree. The effect upon him, as upon Levi, of Christ's presence and call.

When Peter had denied his Lord, we read that Jesus turned, and looked upon him; and, then "Peter remembered the word of the Lord, as he had said: 'Before the cock crow thou shalt deny Me thrice.' And Peter going forth wept bitterly." To the loving sorrow of that look, we may attribute the cause of the Apostle's tears. According to St. Luke, the cock had already crowed, but Peter did not remember the words of Christ, until He turned, and looked upon him. (Lk 22:60-62)[4]

Again, in the Acts, when we read of St. Paul's conversion, we see clearly its instrumental cause in the light, which shined about him, and the voice from heaven: "Saul, Saul, why persecutest thou Me?" (Acts 9:4)

But in the conversion of the Good Thief, it was otherwise. "He had seen no miracles," says St. Leo, "for then had ceased the healing of the sick, the giving light to the blind, the raising of the dead; those other wonders, about to be wrought, had not yet begun; but, nevertheless, he proclaims as Lord and King, Him Who seems to be (no more than) his fellow sufferer."[5] Through what outward means, then, did grace penetrate into his soul? I give here the various answers of the holy doctors and fathers of the Church.

Some find it in the sublime lesson of patience, given by our divine Lord, in the midst of His sufferings, and of the outrages poured upon Him, by the soldiers and the whole Jewish people. Dismas had observed this God-like behavior with ever-increasing wonder and surprise; but his astonishment turned into worshipful admiration, when he heard the Lord asking pardon for those, who were causing His death. "This divine prayer," says the learned Bishop of Bosra, "was probably the instrumental cause of the Thief's conversion, by exciting him to true contrition of heart."[6]

The Cardinal Bishop of Ostia, St. Peter Damian, attributes his conversion to the prayers of the Blessed Virgin. "It is not, indeed, surprising that she, the refuge and help of sinners, should have commenced her ceaseless intercession, even at the foot of the Cross. Standing at the right hand of the Cross of her divine Son, she was placed exactly between Him and the Thief — between the Judge and the criminal; between the Redeemer and the captive slave. What more natural than that she, the mother of mercy, should have asked and obtained, pardon for Dismas, of the dying Savior?" The learned Padre Raynaldus shares and expresses the same opinion.

The celebrated John of Carthagena refers both the prayer of our Lady and the mercy of Christ to the meeting in the desert, of which we spoke at the beginning of this book. He says: "Jesus and Mary, remembering the kindness with which Dismas had treated them at the time of their flight into Egypt, now determined to repay him, by leading him, from the broad way of hell, into the narrow path of salvation. Mary begged for him the grace of forgiveness, and Jesus bestowed it with a generosity worthy of Him Who does not let even a glass of cold water go without its reward."[7]

Others, among whom we will content ourselves with mentioning the learned Spinelli, believed that the instrumental cause of the Good Thief's conversion was to be found in the life-giving influence of the shadow of the Savior's body, which fell upon him at the moment when, being raised upon the cross,

Christ uttered those divine words: "Father, forgive them, for they know not what they do."

The great St. Vincent Ferrer adopts and confirms this tradition. "It may be asked," he says, "why, of the two thieves crucified together with Christ, one was converted, and not the other. Many give answer that the shadow of our Lord's right arm fell upon the Good Thief and changed his heart. They reason thus: If the shadow of St. Peter had in it a healing virtue, which cured the sick of their infirmities (as we read in the fifth chapter of the Acts) how much more should the shadow of Christ have had influence for healing even the soul of the Good Thief?"[8]

Cornelius à Lapide cites these words of St. Vincent Ferrer, and develops the argument they contain.[9] Another argument of the same kind may be found in the well-authenticated fact of persons having been cured through means of the shadow of the Cross itself.[10] If the shadow of the wood has in it such healing power, how much more the shadow of Him Who sanctified that wood, and from Whom all power is derived?

According to this opinion, to which the authority of its defenders lends considerable weight, it would appear that the darkness which overspread the whole earth, at the time of our Lord's crucifixion, did not begin immediately upon His being lifted up; and also that the Cross was so placed that His face was turned towards the west. Now, as regards the darkness, the Gospel tells us that it lasted from the sixth to the ninth hour, but it is nowhere said that it began at the first moment of the sixth hour. It would rather seem, from the number of people passing and repassing Calvary after our Lord's crucifixion, that the darkness did not commence at once. However this may be, there is certainly nothing in the sacred text, to prevent our supposing that there was a short interval of light, during which the shadow of the Lord may have fallen upon Dismas, and may have caused his conversion, with that wondrous rapidity, which beseems Him, Who created the world in an instant, by a single word.[11]

The tradition, which represents our Lord to have been turned towards the west, has a threefold claim upon our respect.

It is venerable by its antiquity, by the testimony of those who have handed it down to us, and by the mysterious sense it contains. As early as the fifth century, we find it in the beautiful poem composed by Sedulius on the Life and Death of Christ.[12] Later on we find it in the writings of St. John Damascene, of Venerable Bede, of Peter de Natalibus, of Spinelli, of Molanus, and many others.[13]

One of the chief witnesses to this tradition, is the great Spanish theologian, Lucas Tudensis, who is, at the same time, the best interpreter of its hidden meaning. "According to what we learn," he says, "from the verses of Sedulius, when our Lord, in dying, stamped the world with the sign of His Cross, (the back of His head was turned towards the east, His feet towards the west, His right hand was stretched out to the north, and His left to the south. From this position we may gather the dignity of the west. For on the cross, the Savior of the World had His face turned westward. Towards the west it was, that, bowing down His head, He gave up the ghost. By the sacrifice of His Body and the shedding of His Blood, He, the eternal High Priest, did consecrate the whole earth, but more especially the western regions; for there it was that He intended to establish the mighty, indestructible, seat of His Vicar, to whom He had given the command that he should feed His lambs and His sheep.

"Satan seems, as it were, to have foreseen the establishment of this surpassing dignity, against the power of which his fiercest efforts might never prevail. Hurled down from the heights, where he had striven to fix his throne, in defiance of the Most High, he yet did not own himself vanquished. As time went on, and the western city of Rome became the capital of the world, she became also the capital of Satan. Stained with every crime and abomination, she succeeded in imposing her yoke, and his, upon all the nations. Our Lord, who had mounted the Cross to do battle with the Prince of Darkness, had also chosen Rome for His own; and in dying He bowed His head towards her to signify that, by His death, He was about to drive out of his chief stronghold the king and god of this world, whose spoils He would take, and the arms wherein he trusted; and to show also that His enemy's shattered altars were soon to become the footstool of His own high Throne.

"It was toward the same western quarter that the Savior's side was opened by the lance and that the Blood and Water flowed forth: the Water destined to cleanse and purify Rome and the world she had soiled, and stained, by her wickedness; the Blood, which was to renew and cleanse this queen of cities, and transform her into a lightsome, burning center of the knowledge and of the love of God. To show forth this design and perfect His work, the divine Redeemer is about to send, from all parts of the world, disciples, who shall wash with their blood, and consecrate to the King of Glory every stone of this city.

"From Judea will come Peter, the prince of the apostles; Cilicia will send Paul, the apostle of the nations; Spain will be represented by the Deacon Lawrence; countless multitudes of martyrs shall come hither from every land. The Prince of Darkness had brought together, and heaped up in this city, all the treasures that the earth produces; the most precious stones and marbles, gold and silver, all wrought and fashioned, by the highest art the world had seen. All these things had been put to the vilest uses, for the worship of devils. But now has come One stronger than he, the True Light, even the Son of God, and He shall take his spoils and give them to his apostles and martyrs, so that what had served for the idolatrous orgies of pagan Rome, shall henceforth serve for the glorious worship of the Church of Christ. Thus had Satan labored to gather together riches, little doubting to what use they should one day be put."[14]

Let us add that it was because of this position of our Lord, in looking toward the west, when nailed upon the Cross, that the early Christians always turned eastward for prayer. Hence, also, the eastward position of our churches.

We have faithfully given the various opinions of the holy fathers and doctors of the Church concerning the outward or instrumental causes of the Good Thief's conversion. We leave it to others to judge between them. For ourselves — whether there was only one such outward cause, or whether all, we have mentioned, concurred together in the effecting of this stupendous miracle — we would rather admire than criticize; and would earnestly call upon all men to fall down and worship the infinite wisdom and power of Him, Who overrules all things for the working out of His own merciful ends.

CHAPTER 14

The Wondrous Nature of the Good Thief's Conversion

MONG the many eruptions of Mount Vesuvius, that of the 2nd of August, 1707, was, if not the most terrific, at least one of the most remarkable. Early in the morning the volcano had begun throwing out dense clouds of smoke and ashes. By mid-day these clouds had thickened and spread to such an extent that the sun was hid from view, and the town of Naples was plunged in darkness like that of a winter's night. The only light visible was the glare of the flames vomited forth from the crater, at the same time as huge stones and streams of boiling lava. A noise as of ceaseless thunder added to the horror and terror of the inhabitants of the city. It was feared that the burning ashes would set fire to the houses, if even they escaped being buried altogether like Pompeii and Herculaneum of old.

Happily, the people of Naples are Christian, and knew that their only hope was prayer. As one man, the whole population rushed to the tomb of their patron, St. Januarius, and claimed his intercession, and not in vain; for in a few moments the eruption was over, the lava ceased to flow, the stones and ashes fell no more, the darkness vanished, and the sun shone forth in dazzling splendor from out a cloudless sky.[1]

Such startling, sudden, changes as this are as rare in the moral, as in the physical order of things, and, wherever they occur, we look upon them as supernatural, or miraculous. In the history of the Church, we occasionally read of men, and women, too, whose early years have been stained with every sort of wickedness, but who, later on, became models of the highest and noblest virtue. But all such changes are miracles of grace, for it is written: "A young man according to his way, even when he is old will not depart from it." (Prov 22:6) Better than any other, the Good Thief exemplifies this exceptional change.

Until now, the life of Dismas has been enveloped, as it were, in blood-stained darkness. To us, as to his contemporaries, he has appeared as a most dangerous brigand; as a criminal whose whole life was made up of a series of robberies and murders; as a wild beast, drunk with blood — the terror of the country, and a disgrace to humanity, now, at last, justly receiving the reward of his crimes, in the most shameful and cruelest of deaths.

"Was there ever a creature so miserable as this robber?" asks St. Chrysostom; "and, suddenly, in the twinkling of an eye, he attains the greatest happiness. He had committed hundreds of murders, his life had been spent in wickedness. As many, as witness his death, accuse his crimes. And yet now he is made blessed, because during a few seconds of time he had feared God, as God ought to be feared."[2]

Whence the change? A sound of that Voice, which breaks the cedars and makes the mountains tremble, had found its way into the heart of the thief; and this heart of stone had been changed into a heart of flesh; the heart of a brute had become that of a man; and the heart of this infamous sinner had been transformed into that of a saint. A ray of the Sun of Justice had fallen upon his countenance, and his whole body had become lightsome. His hideous deformity had given place to superhuman beauty, even angelic grace; and his mouth, which had been full of blasphemies, now uttered words sweet as honey, pleasant as the lowly violet.

Such is this admirable metamorphosis of Calvary: a wolf became a lamb, a blasphemer turned into an evangelist, a vile criminal transformed into one of the greatest of saints! How different this from the obscene and ridiculous metamorphoses of pagan mythology! How much more worthy of study and admiration.

Let us now strive to realize, in so far as we are able, the glorious splendor of our saint's conversion. Let us consider the mysterious nature of his connection with the Son of God, Whose divinity he alone proclaimed. Let us look with the eye of faith towards our Savior, hanging for our sakes upon the Cross. He is surrounded by a multitude of blasphemers, who load Him with insults and reproaches. He is reduced to the last extremity; He is verily become a worm and no man — the outcast of the people. And yet this is the moment He has chosen for showing forth the power of His Godhead. All Nature bears Him witness. The sun refuses its light, and darkness spreads over the whole earth, and the rocks are rent, and the earth quakes, and the graves are opened, and many bodies of the saints arise, and the veil of the Temple is rent in twain from the top even to the bottom.

Now, seeing the earthquake and the things that were done, the centurion and they that were with him, watching Jesus were on the point of being converted, and of crying out: "Indeed this was the Son of God." But in order to show forth still more perfectly the power of Christ, it was necessary that there should be some miracle of the moral order, as striking as these other, physical wonders. In His infinite wisdom, our Lord chose the most difficult of all: the sudden, perfect, and heroic conversion of the worst of sinners.

Speaking on this theme, so often and so grandly sung by the fathers of the Church, St. Chrysostom says: "While upon the Cross, the Lord worked two stupendous miracles. He opened Heaven, which had been closed to men during four thousand years; He brings into it a robber! 'This day,' He says to him, 'thou shalt be with me in Paradise.' What sayest Thou, Lord? Thou art crucified, nailed to a shameful gibbet, and Thou dost promise Paradise! 'Yea, I make this promise to show that I am all-powerful, even while hanging upon the Cross. I have chosen this to show forth My omnipotence — not while I was raising the dead, or commanding the winds and waves, or putting the devils to flight; but now that I am crucified, pierced with nails, despised and spat upon; now, it is, that I transform the soul of the thief.' Thus is the power of the Lord made manifest: His rule over both the moral, and the material, world. He makes the earth to tremble and quake; the rocks are rent asunder; and He calls to Himself and honors the soul of the thief, which until now was assuredly harder than the stone."[3]

Now if, as St. Thomas teaches, the conversion of a sinner is a greater thing than the creation of Heaven and earth,[4] what shall we say of the conversion of Dismas, which was so incomparably greater than any other conversion that it is said to stand alone, and unrivalled.[5]

Surpassing great was the grace, which changed Mary Magdalen, the public sinner, into one of the noblest saints the world has ever seen. So great was it that St. Gregory does not hesitate to say: "Thus it is most sure that God has made two great lights — two Marys, Mary, the mother of the Lord, and that other Mary, the sister of Lazarus. The greater is the Blessed Virgin, whom he has made to rule the day — that is, to give light to the pure and innocent; the other lesser light is the penitent Magdalen, who is ever at the feet of the Blessed Virgin (as a model for sinners, to enlighten them, during the night of their spiritual darkness).[6]

Was not, therefore, the conversion of Magdalen more wonderful than that of the Good Thief? With the devout and learned Orilia, we answer unhesitatingly, No! And for this reason, that, as tradition tells us, she had, before her conversion, witnessed a most tremendous miracle — even that of the raising of the widow's son to life.

The young man's soul as well as his body had been saved from death. He had come back to earth, after having seen the torments of hell. Thenceforward, he was instant in calling upon others to avoid the punishment he had himself so narrowly escaped; so that his death became the seed of life unto many. Of that number, was Mary Magdalen who, filled alike with hope and fear, determined to implore the Savior's mercy. The Good Shepherd is never far off from His erring sheep — and Mary had no difficulty in finding Him where He sat at meat, in the house of Simon, the leprous Pharisee.[7]

It is not our purpose, to examine into the beauty of Magdalen's conversion. Rather would we compare it with that of the Good Thief. She, we have said, was convinced of the Lord's power by the sight of an astounding wonder; but the Good Thief had no such proof. On the contrary, everything he saw was of a nature to shake, not to inspire, belief. He had not known our Lord, during His public life, when He had gone about doing good — healing the sick, casting out devils, feeding the multitudes, raising the dead. He had not heard Him preach the Gospel. He saw Him now for the first time, save that other meeting in the desert, long since forgotten. And to what a state had our sins, and the hatred of the Jews, reduced Him! Yet, notwithstanding all, he recognizes Him, and proclaims Him, God and King! When others have betrayed and deserted Him; when the crowds mock and revile; in the midst of torments and shame; Dismas believes, prays, and worships.[8]

Yea, once again, the conversion of the Magdalen is great and wonderful. No less admirable is that of St. Paul; yet greater than either, and more worthy to be praised, is the conversion of the Good Thief. Let us compare that of the persecutor, with that of the robber. When Saul went forth on his journey to Damascus, breathing out threatenings and slaughter against the disciples of the Lord, he was, perhaps, as far off from Christianity, as the brigand, who knew not God. In his epistles, the Apostle frequently compares himself to the reprobate heathen. Yet this was speaking from out of the depths of his humility; for, in truth, the life of a strict Pharisee was far removed from that of a murderous thief, and Saul was, certainly, never a hypocrite. Be this, however, as it may, it was not until he had been struck to the ground, and had heard a voice from Heaven, that he yielded himself, a captive to Christ. The miracle of his conversion was nevertheless so great, that it has served as a demonstration of the truth of the Christian religion.

Now, let us turn to the Good Thief, and see how much more direct the action of grace was upon him, than upon the Apostle. No heavenly light had struck him with physical blindness, for the sake of opening the eyes of his soul. He had heard no voice proclaiming Jesus of Nazareth — no voice save that of the Jews, insulting, blaspheming, and deriding Him, as a seducer and a malefactor. No man led him to the disciples of the Lord. He had no teacher, such as the kindly Ananias.

I ask again, is it not more wonderful that Dismas should have discerned the Godhead, in a man, dying the most shameful of deaths, than that Saul should have worshipped, and obeyed Christ, after he had heard Him speak, from out a cloud of glory? In the one case, there was a clear manifestation of the power of God; in the other, nothing but the weakness and shame of the most abject of men. May we not fitly, here, repeat with the Apostle, as the sole explanation of this wonder, that the grace of God is all-sufficient; for on Calvary, indeed, was strength made perfect in infirmity.

Shall we now speak of the conversion of Peter? It, also, was sudden, sincere and perfect. But Peter had been, for three years, continually with the Lord. He had been the companion of His vigils, the witness of His miracles. He had confessed Him to be the Christ — the Son of God, and He had received from Him the keys of the Kingdom. He had promised to die with Him and had been fed with His life-giving Body and Blood.

Thrice he denied his Lord — but then Jesus, turning, looked upon him: and who could have resisted the tender reproach of that look? It seemed to say — if, with feeble tongue, we may reverently strive to interpret it — "Is it thus, Peter, thou valuest my love? Is it thus, thou repayest my manifold favors and blessings? A little while past, thou wast ready to go with Me to prison and to death; and, now, thou knowest Me not! Alas! it was good for thee to be with Me upon Thabor, when thou didst taste of My glory — but thou canst not drink the bitter cup of Calvary!

Yet, have I prayed for thee, that thy faith fail not. Be thou converted — confirm thy brethren!" Who could have resisted such an appeal made by the kindest of Masters — the most loving of Friends — even the Son of God?

Such was the instrumental cause of Peter's conversion: but, with Dismas, how different! How different, also, his past life! Instead of living with Christ, he had dwelt among thieves. In place of divine miracles, he had witnessed nothing, but human crime. He had never heard of God, much less of His Anointed. He had never been made clean, nor fed with angel's food. When at last his eyes were opened and he knew that his fellow sufferer was his God, might he not have contented himself with weeping for his past sins, and so, silently, asking pardon of them? This would have been enough, to save him; but, not enough, to satisfy the cravings of his new-born love.

Now far be it from me, to say aught that might tend to disparage the true and perfect conversion of the Prince of the Apostles; but, yet, in comparing it with the conversion of the Good Thief, I cannot fail to note that Peter did not thereupon return, and confess his Divine Master, before the servant of the High Priest, who had heard him curse and swear that he "know not the Man." He nowise retracted his denial; nor did he follow his Lord, on the way to Calvary. Whereas, Dismas bore witness to Christ, even upon the Cross; declared His innocence; rebuked those who outraged and blasphemed Him; and, while confessing his own guilt and the justice of his punishment — in the face of countless foes — proclaimed Him, Lord and God.

As we have already hinted, the circumstances and mode, of the Good Thief's life, ought not to be left out of sight, when we strive to measure the glories of his conversion, and the almighty, irresistible action of the divine mercy upon his soul. Those other great converts, of whom we have spoken, had not been plunged in evil and spiritual darkness, from their youth upward. They had been taught true doctrine and the precepts of virtue, and, more or less, they had, for a time at least, modeled their lives upon them. Now those days of purity and goodwill remained to them — even after their fall — as so many stones, as it were, overthrown, indeed, and scattered, yet ready to be placed again in the new foundation; so that their past furnished *materials* for the building up, in them, of the temple of God, not *obstacles* thereto.

But, with the Good Thief, we find nothing of the sort. Born among robbers, he was steeped in crime, from his very childhood. Around him, he saw only murder and pillage. No means were taken for cultivating or enlightening his intellect, nor training his heart. Not a single ray of light, whether human or divine, ever penetrated the thick darkness of his ignorance. Not a day passed without some gross sin — few, even, without a trace of blood. St. Chrysostom reckons his murders by the thousand, and all we know of him, only helps to make us understand how great was his conversion. It was nothing less than the changing of a brute into a man, that, so, he might become a saint; or, in the words of Holy Writ, it was as hard as for an Ethiopian to change his skin. To man, indeed, the change would have been clearly impossible, but not so with the power of God. "All the waters of the ocean," says Padre Orilia, "would not suffice to whiten the skin of the Ethiopian, or to wash out the spots of the leopard. So it is with man. When he has made to himself, as it were, a second nature of vice, and has been so long plunged in wickedness as to have prevented the development of the moral sense, or stifled it in its birth, it is impossible for him to change his life, unless he be worked upon by a miracle of the divine grace. So it was with Dismas, and such, his conversion."[9]

In a moment, in the twinkling of an eye, this degraded being was rescued from the abyss of sin and lifted up to the greatest height of perfection; he was instantly cleansed from every stain; changed, transformed, and clothed about with virtue. And so perfect was the work of grace that nothing remained for him to do. No penance was required of him; he had not even to pass through the purgatorial flames. At once he was made fit to enter into the joys of Paradise.[10]

"The mercy of God," exclaims St. Chrysostom, "had done everything. For what had this robber said or done? Had he fasted, and wept, and afflicted his body, and done penance during a long time? Nothing of all this. But on the cross itself, immediately after the sentence of death, he received his pardon. See with what speed he was transferred from the cross to heaven. In the midst of torment, he found salvation.[11]

We may, I think, safely conclude that, in the conversion of the Good Thief, the grace of God is shown forth with an incomparable splendor. It is, in the moral order, no less than the creative *fiat*, the masterpiece of the right hand of God. Before this consoling and encouraging miracle, all others seem to fade into nothingness. " *Hujus latronis penitentia non extat æqualis.* "

Unnecessary to add, that the arm of God is not shortened, that His mercy is ever the same. His action at this day is as swift and sure, as it was two thousand years ago. When the waters of baptism touch the head of a child, the soul of that child is instantly made pure and beautiful. Heaven is opened to him, and a place is set apart for him, even among the angels of God, a place of everlasting glory and happiness.

Again, another miracle is daily worked in the sacred tribunal of penance. At the mere word of the priest — spoken in the name — and by the power of God — a soul, black with crime, is made whiter than snow. The sins, which were red as scarlet, are whitened like wool, and are removed from the sinner, as far as the East is from the West. His chains are broken, and hell is shut up which was gaping to receive him. If his contrition is perfect, he is made worthy to be admitted at once into Heaven. How simple the means, how wonderful the effect! How rapid the action of the grace of God! With joy, and confidence, and love, we acknowledge and worship His almighty, infinite Mercy.

CHAPTER 15

Faith of the Good Thief

A S we have already said, the conversion of the Good Thief is a most splendid and glorious example of the mercy of God. It is a no less perfect model of human co-operation. For the conversion of a sinner, it is not enough, that God should speak to his heart. His heart must voluntarily open itself at the divine call, and give itself up to the influence of grace.

So it was with Dismas. The immense favor he had received required of him a corresponding heroic degree of faith, hope, and love. Let us contemplate these virtues which as three suns, light up and beautify his soul; lifting and driving away the dark clouds which heretofore had shrouded it.

The first and most precious ornament of the Church is Faith. Faith holds the highest rank among all the virtues; the rest follow in her train, and without her it is impossible to enter into the Heavenly Kingdom.[1] Faith is the beginning and only sure foundation of the supernatural life. Now faith consists in believing what we cannot see: *Argumentum non apparentium.* And the higher, and more difficult of understanding the truths of revelation, the greater, and stronger, and more piercing must be our faith.

In order to the full appreciation of the faith of our saint, it is necessary for us to consider, once more, the circumstances under which it reached such full perfection. Christ was hanging dying upon the cross, abandoned, insulted, despised, a laughingstock to the wise, the reproach of the people. What sign was there of His Godhead, or even of His Kingship? Where was His throne? Where His court, His royal robes, His attendants and ministers, His guard and troops?

For His throne, we find a cross, the instrument of His death! His court is made up of the robbers, His fellow sufferers, and the crowding multitudes around; for royal robes, a miserable rag; His attendants and ministers, the executioners who, after wreaking upon Him their cruel rage, watch His agony with callous mirth; His guards and troops, a few cowardly disciples, who fled away and left Him, at the first approach of danger.

There was nothing, therefore, kingly to be seen on Calvary. Was there anything divine? Outwardly, nothing. Let us therefore compare the faith by which Dismas discerned his God, with that of the patriarchs and prophets. "Abraham," says St. Chrysostom, "believed in God; but so he believed in One, speaking to him from Heaven, or by the mouth of His angels, Himself directly imposing His commands. Moses believed — but it was on Him, Who had spoken to him from out the burning bush, and in the sound of trumpets and with the voice of thunder, which things had sufficed to convert even unbelievers. Isaiah believed; but he had seen God enthroned in glory. Ezechiel believed; but he had seen the Lord seated upon the cherubim. The other prophets likewise believed, but they all had seen and heard God, in so far as it is given to human nature (to see and hear Him). I say not these things for the sake of undervaluing the saints. God forbid! I speak them for the sake (of enhancing the glory) of him, who by a word alone was made worthy of Paradise."[2]

It is indeed true that Dismas also saw the Lord: but how and when? "In the shame of the cross!" answers the same holy doctor. "He saw Him, not upon His glorious throne, surrounded by the mighty legions of the heavenly host, but upon the cross — and only upon the cross. What do these words signify? They mean that he saw Him upon a mock throne, a thousand times more likely to hide than to reveal His divinity. They mean that, in place of the cherubim and the seraphim, two thieves were His visible companions. They mean that, instead of being worshipped, He was the object of insult and blasphemy. Ah! when I have said he saw Him upon the Cross, and upon the Cross only, I have said all that it is possible to say."[3]

If at least Dismas had heard our Savior utter some authoritative words — something which even asserted His kingly power; if he had heard Him pronounce against His murderers the sentence which He will one day pass upon them, as judge of the quick and the dead, then, at least, we might understand how he recognized Him as the living God. But no; he sees Him only when the powers of Hell are let loose upon Him — when He is delivered up into the hands of the Prince of Darkness. Far from giving sentence against His murderers, He prays for their forgiveness.

Humanly speaking, there was nothing in all this to open the eyes of the Good Thief. In the sight of reason, on the contrary, everything seemed to encourage and increase in him that darkness of error, which so blinded his obstinate comrade, as to make him fall into the impenetrable darkness of hell. Yet it was in the midst of circumstances like these that Dismas, with heroic faith, discerned the Godhead of Christ, and hailed Him King, begging of Him a remembrance when He should have entered into His Kindom! "What!" cries out St. Chrysostom, "thou seest Him crucified, and dost thou proclaim Him King? He is hanging upon the wood, and thou speakest of the Kingdom of Heaven."[4]

We have compared the faith of the Good Thief with that of the patriarchs and prophets; we will now compare it with that of the apostles. "We know and have believed that Thou art the Christ, the Son of God." (Jn 6:69) When was it that their faith was strong enough to give such noble testimony as we find in these words? It was after long enjoyment of the presence and teaching of the Lord; after seeing Him work countless miracles.

They had seen Him, the Creator of all things visible and invisible, commanding the winds and the waves. They had seen

Him change water into wine, feed five thousand men with five loaves and two little fishes, cleanse the lepers, cure the paralytic, give sight to the blind, hearing to the deaf, and speech to the dumb. They had seen Him raise the dead, and put the devils to flight. They had even heard those very devils give witness to His divinity. Again they had seen Him on Thabor, transfigured before them. There, once more, they heard the Voice from Heaven, which — as at the time of His baptism — proclaimed Him the well-pleasing Son of God. Moses and Elias, too, were there, by their presence also exhorting them to hear Him, Who was the end of the law and the prophets, the desired of nations, the Savior of mankind.

Is it surprising that miracles such as these, of which some or all the apostles were witness, should have at last given to their faith the most intense and burning fire? And yet, after all, their faith was hardly so lively as that of Dismas. Even after His resurrection, our Lord was continually rebuking them for their incredulity and hardness of heart. (Mk 16:14; Lk 24:25) To one of them He said, "Because thou hast seen Me, Thomas, thou hast believed. Blessed are they that have not seen and have believed." (Jn 20:29)[5]

These words of our Lord suggest the comparison between the Apostles and our Thief. They had seen and believed: he had not seen, yet had he believed. He had seen neither signs nor wonders. He had not heard the preaching of our Lord, nor the testimony of those He had healed or miraculously fed. None had announced to him the power or the glory of the Messiah. But he had seen Him scoffed, and scourged, and spat upon; treated as a fool, a seducer, an impostor, and a malefactor; and as such condemned to death, by the voice of His own nation. Since our Lord's departure from the Prætorium, nothing had taken place which was calculated to enlighten Dismas, any more than his companion or the accompanying crowd. Yet the faith of our saint was such that it pierced through the thick veil and recognized the Divinity of our Lord, though hidden within His torn and bleeding humanity. He believed that the most abject of men was none other than the Most High God — the Creator of heaven and earth, the Savior of the world. He was not content with silently worshipping: he also fearlessly confessed his faith.[6]

If the faith of the Good Thief was superior to that of the Apostles in ardor and penetration, it surpassed theirs no less in courage and in strength. Let us examine for a moment the conduct of the Apostles, at the very beginning of the sacred Passion. One of them, the traitor, betrayed Him in the garden; the others all took to flight. Not one said a word in His defence. "Then His disciples, leaving Him, all fled away." (Mk 14:50; Mt 27:56) Peter, indeed, drew his sword and cut off the ear of the servant of the High Priest, and afterwards he followed his Lord to the house of Caiaphas. But what did he there? It would have been better to desert than to deny his Master, and to swear that he knew not the Man. John alone appears to have been faithful to the end. He alone of the Apostles stood by the cross of Christ, but even he said no word of love or of rebuke. Ay, verily, not one of the Apostles spoke; but we find the evangelist of Calvary in the Good Thief.

Let us listen again to St. Chrysostom, the golden-mouthed oracle of the East. He says: "But if one should ask, Whence this great happiness of the thief? What has he done that after death he should deserve Paradise? Desirest thou to hear (in what consists) his merit? While Peter was denying (his Lord) upon earth, the thief confessed (Him) upon the Cross. The chief disciple was not able to endure the threats of a miserable little servant-maid, whereas the crucified thief saw, with the eyes of Faith, the Lord of Heaven (and proclaimed Him such), in face of the multitude, saying: Lord, remember me when Thou comest into Thy Kingdom?"[7]

St. Augustine speaks in the same strain. "What great thing," he asks, "had the Good Thief done that he should pass straight from the cross he had so richly deserved, even into Paradise? Would ye know, in short, the power of his faith? While Peter denied below, he proclaimed above. I say not this to accuse the blessed Peter — God forbid — but to show forth the magnanimity of the thief. The disciple dared not brave the wrath of a little servant girl; but the thief feared not the anger of the whole Jewish people, who surrounded him, mad with rage.

"He is not held back by the outward abasement of his fellow sufferer, but, with the eye of faith, he penetrates beyond and despises these things as mere veils, hiding the truth, and he says: 'Lord, remember me when Thou shalt come into Thy kingdom.' Those fell away, who had seen our Lord raise the dead to life; but the thief believed in Him, when He was hanging on the cross. To such faith, what could be added? I know not, for, in truth, Christ hath not found so great faith in Israel — nay, nor in the whole world."[8]

Eusebius, speaking on the same subject, concludes thus: "Far greater, far more glorious, was it for the Good Thief to believe that a man, dying in the most frightful torment, was the Lord, than if he had believed in Him, when He was working miracles. Ah! It was not, indeed, without cause that he deserved so great a reward."[9]

Need we therefore wonder that the saints should have continually sung the glories of the Good Thief; or that after the Blessed Virgin, St. Peter, and St. Paul, none should have received a larger measure of praise from the fathers and doctors of the Church.[10]

CHAPTER 16

Hope of the Good Thief

MAN is the temple of the Living God, a temple not made with hands, constructed by the power of the Most High. "*Dei ædificatio estis:*"(1 Cor 3:9) Ye are God's building. This is especially true as regards the edifice of the spiritual life. Every building must have foundations. Now the foundation of holiness, is faith. We have seen how strong and perfect was this foundation in the soul of the Good Thief. Let us now examine the superstructure of hope and charity, which we shall find to be in nowise unworthy of its base.

"The House of God," says St. Augustine, "is founded upon Faith, built with Hope, and crowned with Love."[1] And St. Bernard: "It is with good reason, that the apostle defines faith as the substance of things hoped for, for it is plain that no man hopes for things not believed in, any more than he attempts to paint on the void of emptiness. Wherefore Faith says (to us): Unspeakably great are the goods prepared by God for His faithful; and Hope says: 'For me are these things laid up;' and 'Charity, I run to (seize) them.'"[2]

The nature of these three virtues, and their mutual relations, have been defined by St. Thomas with his usual admirable clearness of expression. "There are superadded to the intellect of man, certain supernatural elements (or powers) which comprehend truth, by means of a divine light; and there are matters of belief

111

of which is *Faith*. In the second place comes the will, which reaches forth towards God, and inasmuch as the intention is directed towards Him as to an attainable end, this pertains to *Hope*. But in so far as the will is admitted to a certain spiritual union, by which it is in some sort transformed into that end, this is wrought by *Charity*."

This wonderful spiritual edifice is not often built up in a day; generally, it takes the lifetime of a saint. But, by a rare privilege, in the case of the Good Thief, the great work was done in a moment. In the twinkling of an eye, his hope became perfect, as his faith. Now hope may be said to be perfect, when it is firm and ardent in an heroic degree. Such was that of Dismas.

Hope is firm when nothing can succeed in shaking it, when nothing makes it fear or hesitate, neither the enormity, nor the number of past sins: nor the thought of the dignity of Him offended, nor of the unworthiness of the offender: nor yet the greatness of the looked-for grace. Such hope furnishes a triumphant answer to every rebuff. It even overcomes the apparent resistance of God, if we may so speak. Thus, it says, with Job: "Though (the Lord) slay me, yet will I hope in Him," (Job 13:15) or with the Canaanean woman who, when compared to the dogs, still continued her prayer, saying: "Yea, Lord; for the whelps also eat, under the table, of the crumbs of the children." (Mt 15:29)

Let us now see of what sort was the hope of the Good Thief. He had confessed his guilt, and avowed it such that the most cruel and shameful of deaths was but its due reward. "But we indeed justly." (Lk 23:41) From this abyss of misery, he saved himself by grasping hold of that hope, which, as St. Paul says, is as an anchor of the soul, sure and firm, (Heb 6:19) to which we may fly for safety. With the full strength of his ardent faith, Dismas anchored his hope upon the solid rock of the infinite power and mercy of God.

From that moment he felt no more fear or doubt; calmly and confidently he looked for what he had asked for. And what had he asked for? He had asked for no less than that which the saints have won by a long life of toil and suffering; he asked for the good things God reserves for those that love Him; he asked, in a word, for Heaven — that is, for the everlasting possession and enjoyment of God. "Lord, remember me, when Thou shalt come into Thy Kingdom." That these words bear the interpretation we have put upon them, is clearly shown by our Lord's reply: "This day shalt thou be with Me in Paradise."

Let us consider for a moment who and what is he who thus boldly asks for Heaven — Dismas it is, the notorious robber, grown old in wickedness, whose whole life has been, as it were, one great sin. His mouth is still stained with blasphemies, and yet he dares make such a request as this! "What courage!" exclaims St. Bernard.[3] We had almost said: "What audaciousness!" But yet his trust was not unwarranted, he obtained the wished-for boon.

O my God, verily, Thy ways are not as our ways, nor Thy thoughts, our thoughts! What we had deemed presumption, Thou namest hope. Thou receivest whom we had rejected. Wonderful, indeed, is Thy mercy, unspeakable Thy loving kindness. Thou deignest to receive, as a pleasing homage, the trustful prayer of one, sunk in the lowest deep of sin. The greater his need, the more complete his utter helplessness, the more powerful does his prayer become, the more claim does it make upon Thy compassionate Heart! Ah! well may we praise Thy name, O Lord, and give thanks to Thee for Thine infinite power, and wisdom, and love.

Aforetime, we find, in the royal Psalmist, a great and striking example of, what we may term, the sinner's claim. He also had committed a great crime, and, being rebuked, did penance for it and was forgiven. Let us observe, however, the singular plea he advances when, in prayer, the thought of his guilt comes back upon him. "For Thy name's sake, O Lord, Thou wilt pardon my sin; for it is great." (Ps 24:11) To forgive a slight injury is but a small thing, a man could do as much, but to forgive some exceeding great crime is reserved for the infinite mercy of God alone.

We have said — and proved, we think — that the hope of Dismas was firm, well-grounded, and sure. We have now to consider its lively, all-pervading strength. When Christian Hope is lively, it influences and subjects every power of the soul and body. With the eyes of faith, it looks ever far beyond the narrow horizon of this present life, even on to that, which God has prepared for those who love Him. It speaks, but its converse is of Heaven: its heart is on fire, but it burns at the thought of things unseen. It makes use of the body, of its hands and feet, and every member; but solely in the interest of the work of Christ. Having God for its object, it stoops to no lesser thing. All that is not Him, it esteems as nothing, as dust and ashes, as very dung. And, yet, not blind, for it makes every means contribute to its One great End; with the mammon of iniquity, it buys for itself the unconsumable treasures. If a thing can serve as a help to salvation, well; but if not, hope disdains it, and, passing by, pitilessly shatters every bar and obstacle.

Like to a bird, which wings its way through the air, regardless of rain and snow, of heat or cold, of clouds and storms and contrary winds — hope sails through the things of time, if sometimes hindered, yet in spite of all; and so, with fixed upward gaze, rests not until it hath reached the heights, even the heights of Sion.

Or, like to those great rivers, that roll their waters oceanwards from distances untold, dashing over rocks innumerable, through unknown regions, making for themselves an ever-widening path, and breaking through what obstacles man or Nature, had placed in their way, so eagerly they speed them, to mingle their torrents with the many waters; even so, hope rushes on to the true Ocean of Delights, nor lets itself be held back, by any human or created thing. It is ever the same: ever full of trust in God, whether in youth or old age; at work or at rest; amid beauty, and riches, and pleasures, or amid poverty, squalor, and misery; in health or sickness; whether honored or reviled; persecuted or at peace. Such hope fainteth not, but, ever lifting its eyes towards the mountain of God, waiteth for Christ, until He come.

When hope is in the highest degree firm and lively, it becomes, what we may call, heroic. Such was the hope of the

Good Thief. He asked not temporal favors from our Lord, neither to be delivered from the cross, nor restored to freedom; but he asked for something far better, when he begged that Jesus should remember him, on coming to His Kingdom. We have seen already, how much was contained in the apparently simple words he uttered. After speaking them, Dismas was happy, for his hope was heroically firm and lively, and he knew that it would not be vain. He knew that God gives us, in His mercy, more blessings than we can ask for or conceive; according to the beautiful prayer of the Church's liturgy: "*Qui pre supplicum excedisces et vota.*"

Now, it seems to us, that the confidence of both Mary Magdalen and St. Peter was less firm and less lively, than that of the Good Thief. Overwhelmed with shame, and remorse, the first came to ask pardon of her sins. She entered the house, of the Pharisee with mingled feelings of hope and fear. She dared not speak to our Lord, nor present herself before Him, but, standing behind Him, she began to wash His feet with her tears, and wiped them with the hairs of her head, and kissed His feet, and anointed them with the ointment.

Peter, after his fall, had not the courage to go and throw himself at his Master's feet, but, forthwith, leaving the scene of his denial, he went forth and wept bitterly. Now, if the confidence of the Apostle had reached the same heroic degree as that of Dismas, he would assuredly have returned among the servants of the High Priest and boldly confessed the divinity of Christ, for he would have had a sure and firm hope that his Lord would give him grace sufficient to enable him to suffer whatever taunts, or scorn, or ill-treatment, his behavior would have exposed him to.

But, what Peter had not ventured to do, the thief did, in the midst of the agonies of death. Full of hope and trust, he proclaimed the innocence of our Lord and the injustice of His sentence: and, fixing his eyes upon the divine Victim, he hesitated not to ask of Him the best gift He had to bestow. His hope was perfect; so was its reward.

Truly has it been said of Dismas: "Suddenly, from being an enemy, he became a friend; a stranger, he became a loving companion; coming from afar, he showed himself the true neighbor; a robber, he was changed into a glorious confessor! Great, indeed, was the confidence of the thief. Conscious to himself of every sort of guilt and sin, without a single redeeming good work, he had passed his lawless life in taking the goods and even the lives of men; yet, at the end of his days, at the very gates of death, when all hopes of this present life were over, he conceived a hope of the life to come, which he had so grievously forfeited, or rather which he had never done anything to deserve. If the thief had cause to hope, who shall henceforth despair?"[4]

CHAPTER 17

Charity of the Good Thief

CHARITY is the crowning of the spiritual edifice. Without charity, faith would be void, and hope vain. We have seen how great was the faith of the Good Thief; how perfect, his hope. Let us now consider the measure of his love. Love tends always to union with its object; so that to love is to unite. When the thoughts of our friend are our thoughts; when his tastes and interests are our interests and tastes; his joys and sorrows, ours; his losses, our losses; and his life forms, as it were, one with our life; then, indeed, is our love, true love. Now charity — the highest form of love — has, so to speak, two hands; with the one it holds fast to God, with the other, it clings to its neighbor. With the first, it raises itself up to its Heavenly Father; with the second, it draws after it its brethren and helps to bring them also to God, our One true End, and lasting reward. Thus, charity fulfils the prayer of Christ, and makes us all one, even as He and His Father are one.

When charity has fully penetrated a soul, and has shown itself by works that require a great and exceptional degree of courage, a courage stronger than death, then do we term such charity heroic. We do not hesitate to describe as such the charity of Dismas.

In the order of Nature, we do not see the sun suddenly leap out of the night and change the darkness into perfect day;

neither does the traveler, with one bound, reach the tops of the mountain; but slowly, and gradually, all things are done. The greatest end has, usually, but a small beginning. And, it is the same, in the order of grace. Hence the maxim: *Nemo repente fit summus.* Perfection is not reached with lightning speed. It is the fruit of much labor — of weary vigils, and fastings, and sufferings, and pain.

But, sometimes, though rarely, God sees fit to dispense with the laws He has made, and thus we occasionally see certain happy souls attain, in a short time, to the greatest height of perfection. In the first rank of these privileged beings, stands the Good Thief. In a moment, in the twinkling of an eye, the seed of grace developed, in him, into the goodly tree of virtue. Nothing was wanting, neither the roots of faith, the stem of hope, nor the flowers and fruits of charity. His whole soul was on fire with the love of God, and so his past sins were burnt away and utterly destroyed.

"On the cross," says St. Gregory, "the hands and feet (of the Good Thief) were held and transfixed by the nails; nothing in him was left free, save his heart and his tongue. Inspired by God, he offered up to Him all he had to dispose of: with his heart he believed in justice, his tongue proclaimed it. According to the testimony of the Apostle, there are three chief virtues which must dwell in the hearts of the faithful; and these are faith, hope, and charity. On a sudden, being filled with grace, the thief received these (virtues into his soul), and he preserved them upon the cross."[1]

The other fathers speak in the same sense. Let us now listen to the seraphic St. Bernardine of Siena. He says of Dismas: "All that he had, he offered up to Jesus, as a sacrifice of perfect love. Crucified, he could no longer make use of his hands and feet; his heart and tongue alone were free. He offered them both: the first as a sacrifice of sweet-smelling odor, burnt by the flames of love; the second as the mouth-piece of the first."[2]

What more shall I say? Let me cry out with the blessed Amadeus: "O aromatic, sweet-smelling phœnix, thou art more pleasing, in the presence of the King, than cinnamon, or balm, or the precious spikenard."[3]

The charity which consumed the heart of the Good Thief, inspired his tongue. Herein lies the proof of its heroic perfection. As soon as Dismas had recognized the innocence and divinity of Christ, he understood also the cause of His sufferings. That cause was none other than the sins of men; and truly could the thief say within himself: "I am the worst of sinners. It is for my sake that He drinks the cup of bitterness to the dregs; to save me from everlasting torments, He is covered with wounds from head to foot. He dies to give me life." Or, in the words of a great saint: "The wounds of Christ were not Christ's own wounds, but rather the wounds of sin. So the thief, seeing, as it were, his own wounds in the body of his Lord, loved Him the more."[4]

And such is his love that, forgetting his own sufferings, he thinks only of the sufferings of Jesus, and breaks forth into words of heroic boldness. He takes up the defence of the Messias, and proclaims his innocence; and so doing fears not to brave the hatred and wrath of the assembled synagogue.[5]

"This man hath done no evil. What crimes do you accuse Him of, ye, who have condemned Him — thou, Pilate, who didst expressly declare His innocence, and ye, Annas, Caiaphas, priests and ancients of the people? Was it a crime to preach to you the kingdom of God, and His love to men? Was it a crime to heal your sick, to raise your dead? Was it a crime to convert sinners, to comfort the afflicted, to feed the poor, to deliver those possessed? For which of these things is it, that ye have outraged and insulted Him, spat upon Him, covered Him with wounds, and nailed Him to the shameful cross? I and my companion, indeed, are guilty, and we are rightfully condemned; but He, Jesus of Nazareth, hath done no evil." All this, and much more, was contained in those few words of the Good Thief: "This man hath done no evil." Who can fail to admire such generous courage?

"Let us examine carefully," says a pious hermit, "what manner of man was this robber — lest, being ignorant of the cause of his hope, we should fall into the sin of presumption. All the friends, and neighbors, and kinsmen, and even the disciples of our Lord had left Him and fled. As it had been foretold: "I will strike the shepherd, and the sheep shall be dispersed." Even the disciple, whom Jesus loved, had not remained with Him all the time of His passion. The Apostles seemed one and all to have forgotten the many signs and wonders they had witnessed, and the power of doing things yet even greater, which their Master had given them. But while the Apostles deserted Him Whom they had previously confessed, the robber, who had not known Him during life, confessed Him, now that He was at the point of death."[6] His faith and courage being such, we need not wonder at the greatness of his hope, nor at its reward.

As we have said, charity has two hands. With the one, Dismas seized hold of, and clung on to Christ, his Savior; with the other, he strove to take hold of his fellow sufferer for the sake of bringing him to God, so that, after having shared his crimes and punishment, he might also share the never-ending happiness he so confidently hoped for, for himself.

Fear is the beginning of wisdom — Dismas therefore turned all his efforts towards awakening fear in the heart of his companion. "Neither dost thou fear God?" he asked him reproachfully. Thou art about to die — yet fearest thou not Him Who is about to judge thee? Surely we were guilty enough already, thou needst not add to thy past sins this new guilt; thou needst not insult and blaspheme the Just.

Then, as a skilful preacher, the Good Thief addresses himself even to the weakness of his compeer; he touches his self-love. Wherefore, he says, dost thou insult Him? Dost thou not see that every word thou sayest against Him falls back with tenfold force upon thyself; seeing thou art under the same condemnation? But we indeed justly; for we receive the due reward of our deeds. Moreover, if our companion were guilty, as indeed He is innocent, it would be mean and cowardly to insult Him, now that He is in the midst of torments.

But He is not only innocent: He is holy; He is very God! He is dying for us both: for all mankind. Be not so blind as to refuse to acknowledge Him for what He is. It is not too late — repent thee of thy sins; ask pardon and thou shalt obtain it. I have found the true way that leadeth unto life everlasting — come, let us journey on together on the new road, as we did on the old; but if not, we shall be for ever separated, for thy road leadeth to destruction.[7]

Unhappily, we know that the words of the Good Thief fell upon the hard rock — that they failed altogether to effect the conversion of his companion. But his charity was all the more meritorious, in that it received no reward in this world. He risked much, and, apparently, gained nothing; for in rebuking and exhorting his fellow sufferer, Dismas took upon him to defend our Lord, and thus drew down upon himself the wrath and hatred of the Jews, who were not slow to wreak their vengeance upon him. For this reason it was that, as tradition tells us, Dismas was the first of the thieves to have his legs broken. In this way his enemies were able at once to punish and to silence him.

With Venerable Bede, I ask once again: "Who can help admiring the heroic charity of this thief?"[8] I say more; let us not be content with barren admiration, let us strive — each one in our own sphere and measure — to reproduce in ourselves what we admire in him.

CHAPTER 18

Prudence and Justice of the Good Thief

WE have already seen in what high degree the Good Thief was possessed of the three theological virtues: Faith, Hope, and Charity. We will now endeavor to show that the cardinal virtues were not behind in hand in the work of his sanctification; but that, on the contrary, his prudence, justice, fortitude, and temperance were in no wise less perfect than his faith, and hope, and love.

The prince of theologians, St. Thomas Aquinas, defines prudence as, "*a good counselor*, to be consulted in all things pertaining to the life of man, and to the great End of that life."[1] We must, however, distinguish between the virtue of prudence and its counterfeit, worldly craftiness, which has improperly usurped the same name. Such false prudence is either earthly and animal, or it is devilish. It may help a man to enrich and advance himself; it may enable him to realize his ambition; but in so doing it destroys his best happiness, for, in the search after the goods of this world, he loses sight of those of the world to come. All his life long, Dismas had been under the influence of this false prudence. He had been a successful robber, and had often escaped human justice. But at last he had been overreached, and he was now paying the penalty — a few moments more, and he would have passed from the agonies of the cross to the everlasting torments of hell.

But suddenly, he was converted, and true prudence entered his soul, together with that glorious company of virtues we have already described. At once it showed itself in the examination he made of his past life, in the consequent confession of his guilt, and in the prayer which he addressed to our Lord. Dismas no longer deceived himself. He began to understand what it is to die. He saw that there remained to him but a few seconds of what is commonly called life, but which is, in reality, nothing better than a living death. Without hesitation, he turned his thoughts towards that life which is alone worthy of the name — the life which begins on the other side of the grave, and which is to everlasting.

By the light of the divine virtue of prudence, Dismas saw at once the means he must make use of to obtain eternal life. He was enabled to discern the Son of God in the Man who was dying by his side; enabled also to understand the motive of His death. Seeing that He was dying to save mankind, Dismas was only helping Him to realize His object, when he asked of Him salvation. The thought of his crimes humbled him, indeed, and moved him to sorrow, but it could not hold him back; for, however great his sins, he knew that the mercy of his Savior was infinitely greater. He had heard Him pray for those who were putting Him to death, and reviling and blaspheming Him. How much more would He be likely to show mercy to His fellow sufferer, if he asked it of Him.

Human prudence would have pronounced it folly to ask a boon of one he had so lately been insulting; but not so divine prudence. By faith, he had come to know the one true God, in the person of Jesus Christ Whom He had sent; hope had taught him where to put his trust; charity had shown him how to love aright: it remained for prudence to point out to him the best use to make of so much mercy. "This ingenious, clever thief," says St. Gregory of Nyssa, "had perceived the treasure, and, making the most of his opportunity, he possessed himself of life everlasting. A truly sagacious and beautiful use of the art of robbery!"[2]

Prudence did not only suggest to Dismas to ask pardon, but it showed him also how to deserve it. It made him understand that it is necessary to confess the sins we would have forgiven; and so, briefly, he acknowledged that his death was but the just punishment of his crimes. This one word was enough to set forth their heinousness.

St. Chrysostom, in commenting on this proof of exquisite prudence, says: "Listen to his perfect confession! No man suggested it, neither did any force him to make it. Of his own free will he publicly confessed his iniquities, saying: 'We are justly condemned, for we receive the due reward of our deeds, but this Man hath done no evil.' He dared not say 'Remember me in thy Kingdom' until he had first rid himself, by confession, of the load of sin. See, then, what a great thing is confession! The thief confessed, and Paradise was opened to him; he confessed, and thereupon so great a trust and confidence were given him, that, notwithstanding a life of crime, he was enabled to ask a kingdom."[3]

In his mode of asking, we see fresh evidence of the divine virtue of prudence. He earnestly desired eternal life, but how dared he ask for it? True, that with exceeding great humility, he had made confession of his sins. True, again, that he, and he alone, had taken upon himself to vindicate the innocence of our Lord. Yet would he say to himself: How is it possible that, after such a life as mine, Heaven should be given me at the very first sign of repentance? Does God make so little account of His Kingdom as to be willing to bestow it on one so unworthy, for the mere asking? Some such thoughts as these must surely have passed through the mind of the Good Thief.

But in the midst of his perplexity, prudence came to his aid. Ask little, it said to him, and thou wilt obtain much. God does not stoop to measure His gifts, nor to proportion them to our merits, or even to our prayers. He gives freely, without stint. He loves to give what man had not even thought of asking. For God is good, and He is generous. He is almighty, and His mercy knows no bounds.

In accordance, therefore, with the dictates of prudence, the thief, as we know, asked only a simple remembrance. "Remember me when Thou shalt come into Thy Kingdom." What more humble? "He dared not say," writes St. Lawrence Justinian, "give me the Kingdom; make me to share in Thy glory; but only this — 'Remember me.' He knew himself to be unworthy to enter the eternal Kingdom, for he was a sinner, his heart and hands steeped in guilt. How could he expect to follow where, by the light of grace, he knew that Christ was about to make his triumphal entry."[4]

Prudently, but with firm hope, Dismas had made his request. We shall, presently, consider the gracious answer he received. We share his hope. Oh! let us be equally prudent in striving to imitate his humility. Self-abasement is a magnet which attracts the best gifts of God, as it is written, "he that humbleth himself shall be exalted."

We come, now, to the second of the cardinal virtues. Justice is usually defined as an upright intention of rendering to all, that which is due: to God, everything that we have, since He is Lord of all; and to our neighbor, much, for we are bound to love him as ourselves. Or, as St. Thomas words it: "Justice is that uprightness of mind by which a man does, in every matter, the thing which is right."[5] The whole duty of man consists in love — love of God, and love of his neighbor. Now, justice gives us the measure, in which to fulfill this duty.

First, therefore, we have justice towards God, which may be divided into the four kinds of homage due — homage of praise, because of His great glory and infinite perfections; homage of thanksgiving for His countless gifts; homage of satisfaction for sin, whether of commission or omission; and, finally, homage of repentant sorrow for such of His graces as we may have neglected.[6]

Now, from what we have already said of Dismas, it would seem unnecessary, to show categorically the perfect manner in which he complied with each one of these obligations. Still the love we bear this great Saint, unhappily too little known, obliges us to say a few words on each point of his perfection — even though at the risk of repetition. We will here content ourselves with briefly pointing out that the Good Thief rendered to God all these kinds of homage, by adoring the divinity of Christ as soon as it was made known to him on the cross; by proclaiming, praising, and defending Him from calumny and reproach; by freely confessing his own sins, and acknowledging that he had justly incurred death as their punishment; and by suffering patiently its worst agonies, as an expiation of his guilt. Moreover, by the prayer he addressed to our Lord, Dismas further proclaimed Him as the author of all good, and so fully paid the debt of justice owing to God.

Now, secondly, as regards justice towards his neighbor. This debt, also, he paid to the last farthing. Before all, he repaired the scandal of his evil life by avowing the justice of his chastisement. To all, whether Jews or Romans, Pharisees or publicans, priests or people, he proclaimed the innocence of the Lamb of God; and, by His innocence, His Divinity also — for had He not been the Son of God, He would have been indeed, as they falsely said, an impostor and a seducer. Dismas feared not to speak the truth, at whatever cost. He owed it to God, and he owed it to his neighbor. He did all that in him lay to enlighten and convert those around him — more especially to save that other thief who had been his companion in wickedness, and whom he now longed to gain as his companion in repentance, and everlasting happiness. His was not the fault, if his efforts proved vain. Nor did their apparent failure in any wise diminish his merit or his consequent glory.

When we consider all the circumstances of time and place, we cannot help repeating that the justice of the Good Thief, as well as all his other virtues, seems to us to have reached a perfection so great as to be unsurpassed, if not unrivalled, by that of any other Saint. None other, we may safely say, showed more heroic zeal for the glory of God, and the conversion of souls: more humility, more faith, more trust, more perfect love, at any given moment of his life, than did Dismas in the midst of the agonies of death.

It may not here be out of place, to insert the following eloquent passage, taken from a sermon of the Abbot Godfrey of Vendome: "Four great things were possessed by the thief, who confessed Christ upon the cross — wisdom, which by the light of faith made known to him the divinity of Christ, and, this, when all the disciples had left and abandoned Him; justice, which, through charity, made him rebuke the blasphemies of the other thief; holiness, which enabled him to pray to Christ with faith and love; and, lastly, the reward, for he was given a share in the Redemption, according to the words of our Lord: 'This day shalt thou be with Me in Paradise.'"[7]

CHAPTER 19

Fortitude and Temperance of the Good Thief

TO suffer, and to do, is the sum of human life. For both these things, the virtue of Fortitude is required. Hence the definition of St. Thomas: "Fortitude is that disposition of the soul which strengthens in it what is according to reason, as against the assault of the passions, and the toilsome fatigue of work."[1] Charity is the source and fountain head of this, as it is of all other virtues. Or rather, in the words of St. Augustine: "Fortitude is love which suffers willingly all things for God's sake."[2] So that both virtues really form but one. We have seen the perfection of the charity of the Good Thief. We may thence safely conclude that his fortitude was equally heroic. Nevertheless, we must say a few words of some of the great acts which fortitude enabled him to do.

"From fortitude," says St. Bonaventure, "proceed magnanimity, trustfulness, freedom from care, patience, perseverance, long-suffering, kindness, humility, and meekness."[3]

Magnanimity could not exist without her other sister virtues; but she is at the same time their support and their greatest glory. With a noble, generous courage she leads them by the hand, as it were, and nothing daunted, helps them to undertake things most difficult and most repulsive to human nature, and with a calm, constant, and sublime singleness of aim, enables them to carry them out, in spite of every obstacle.

We find this virtue strikingly developed, in the soul of Dismas. For this virtue it was, which enabled him so bravely, so simply, and so calmly to undertake, himself alone, the defence of our Lord and the conversion of his companion and of the persecuting Jews. This it was, also, which enabled him to endure without murmur the torments of the cross and the shame attendant on that most ignominious form of death. It helped him to do yet more. An avowal of guilt is, perhaps, the hardest of trials to the pride of man. One of the chief causes of the prevalent increase of wickedness is neglect of the sacred tribunal of penance. Ah! if all men would only confess their sins, the face of the earth would be renewed without fail, goodness and purity would increase, and unbelief be done away. But against confession, pride forms an almost impassable barrier. There is nothing more strong than pride — though, at the same time, nothing more weak. Through weakness, man falls into sin; through weakness, also, he dares not confess his guilt. Aye, would to God, that all sinners would imitate the glorious example given us by the Good Thief! Not content with confessing in a low voice, to be heard by our Savior alone, Dismas loudly proclaimed his guilt, and the justice of his punishment; and that, in face of the jeering, howling multitude.

"Trustfulness," says St. Augustine, "makes the soul expect with a sure hope the best and greatest things,"[4] and freedom from care ensures the peace of the soul. "It is itself," as says St. Thomas, "that perfect peace of mind which knows not fear."[5] A great thing, indeed,was the pardon of a long life of wickedness; a still greater, and the best of all, was the reward asked for by the repentant thief, even the kingdom of Heaven. Yet such was his trust that he did not for an instant doubt the firmness and sureness of his confident expectation. Calmly and peacefully he waited for the looked-for blessings, for his soul was free from care and fear.

"Patience," according to St. Bonaventure, "is a virtue which enables us to bear calmly (and cheerfully) all injuries and adversities and shame."[6] The patience of our saint was not less remarkable than his trustfulness and generous courage. His sufferings were most intense, far greater than anything we can ever imagine, yet not a murmur crossed his lips.

The memory of his past life served him as a strong incentive to patience. In acknowledging the justice of his chastisement, he accepted his sufferings as an expiation for his sins. We admire the constancy of the martyrs in the midst of their sufferings; but they, at least, had the comfort of knowing themselves innocent. Their alleged crime was their highest virtue: their faith in Jesus Christ. But this comfort was denied the thief, and the absence of it serves to enhance the merit of his patience.

"Perseverance," says the learned Chancellor Gerson, "is that fortitude which earnestly and unceasingly directs and shapes the works of a man, so that they should not be found wanting in the end."[7] Longanimity is a sort of long-suffering patience, which, from the constancy of its nature, is nearly akin to final perseverance. Both have the task of preparing a man for death — on them his fate depends; for unless a man persevere unto the end, what virtues he had previously exercised through life would avail him nothing.

Now, from the moment of his conversion, Dismas flung aside all doubt and hesitation. His courage never wavered; his faith failed not, nor did his heart grow faint. Once, and forever, he had raised his mind to God. His eyes were firmly fixed upon the everlasting hills. Patiently he bore his sufferings, and was content to bear them, so long as God should will it. And so he persevered, even to the end, and received the glorious crown, together with the martyr's palm.

"True humility," says St. Thomas, "prevents a man setting store by his own virtues, and makes him look to the divine help for all that he requires."[8] Meekness is, so to speak, the twin sister of humility. "Learn of Me," says our Lord, "for I am meek and humble of heart." Now, "meekness is that virtue, which schools the heart to bear patiently all injuries, stripes, and shameful insults."[9] In Holy Writ, the Messias is sometimes named the

Lamb of God, sometimes the Lion of Juda. The one epithet signifies His meekness and humility; the other His kingly strength. The union of these qualities makes up the sum of perfection.

As holiness is the imitation of Christ, so we must look, in His saints, for the shadow of His own divine virtues. We find it very distinct upon the soul of Dismas. Like a lion, he had put forth his strength in defence of his Lord; like a lamb, he had humbled himself in the presence of God, and in the sight of all the people. Humbly, he had avowed his guilt, humbly, he had accepted its penalty. With lowly diffidence of self he hoped and expected all things, from the pure mercy of God. All that he dared ask for was, that the Lord should not forget him.

His self-abasement was the measure of his meekness. What a change had grace worked in his soul! All his life long he had been hard, bloodthirsty, and intensely cruel; but, on the cross, he became a very pattern of gentleness. Silently he bore his sufferings — without complaint. Not a murmur did he utter, amid the most atrocious torments; not a word did he answer to the taunts, and jeers, and reproaches of the crowd.

In conclusion of this part of our subject, we would ask, in the words of an illustrious Cardinal: "Do you wish to see a striking miracle of the power of God? Come, then, and contemplate Dismas, in the glory of his strength. All the Apostles, the chosen sons of grace, had taken flight, leaving their divine Master alone. The Jews were raging around Him, but, nothing daunted, the Good Thief declared His innocence. A prodigy of fortitude, this! And, yet another: Dismas was not ashamed, at the same time, publicly to confess his own guilt, and to acknowledge the justice of its punishment."[10]

We come now to the last of the four cardinal virtues. What is Temperance? We will make answer, with St. Augustine, that a man who possesses this virtue is one who, "in regard to the fleeting and perishable things of this life, strictly follows the rule laid down in both the Old and the New Testament — that is, he loves none of these things for their own sake, neither does he think it lawful to seek after or desire them. But such of them as are necessary to life, or to the requirements of his position, he makes use of, with the moderation of a passing traveler, not with the passion of a lover."[11]

Temperance gives us the true mean, equally far removed from excess and from want. It holds, as it were the balance of the soul, keeping both the scales pretty equally weighted. Its chief office is to repress, and guard against, the ever-surging flood of human pride. Temperance saves the soul both from the ebb and flow of its perilous waters; it raises it far above both discouragement and presumption — those deadly tides, which have washed away so many a fair work of God's.

Long time had Dismas been the slave of pride — as, indeed, of every vice. But, now, he was entirely set free; not a trace left of his former bondage. On the cross his temperance was perfect, keeping him equally far removed from presumption and despair; yet must he have been strongly tempted both to the one and to the other. He was at the point of death — behind him, a life of sin, with nothing to redeem its blackness; before him, the justice of an offended God. This was enough to make him despair, if he had not understood the infinite mercy of the Savior, Who was dying for his sake. But this light had not shined upon him in vain; it had shown him the enemy, and he had defeated him, and vanquished pride had given place in his heart to the sweetest confidence in God.

But, having been saved from the abyss of despair, there was great danger lest, being pardoned, the Good Thief should be tempted to sin by presumption of God's mercy. Not so, however; for that perfect love, which had enabled him to conquer pride in the first instance, enabled him also to withstand its fresh assault. Dismas loved Christ for His own sake, and not because of His gifts. His love was no mean, selfish love; he desired henceforth the glory of God — not his own advancement. If he asked for Heaven, it was not so much to avoid hell, as to make sure that he would never offend God more, or lose the privilege of His love. Hence the lowliness of his humble prayer. "See," says St. Bernard, "see, the temperance of this thief. He does not say: 'Make me happy,' but he asks only what may be pleasing, in the sight of God. He says merely:

'Remember me.'"[12]

We trust that we have said enough in this, and the foregoing chapters, to prove conclusively that the Good Thief was fully possessed of each of the seven great virtues, an heroic degree of which is necessary to that perfection of holiness, to which the Church sets her seal, by bulls of canonization. Such virtues must always excite our admiration; but, in this case, they do so in an uncommon degree, from the wonderful contrast they form in the soul of the thief to his previous wickedness. That very wickedness, now that it is done away, tends to show forth more clearly — in high relief as it were — the wonder-working power of divine grace.

Yea, God is always surpassing great, and we must fall down and worship Him, wherever we see Him revealed; for He is admirable in all His works — admirable, when, on the first day of creation, He commanded the light to be, and the light was; admirable, when, in the power of His might, He drew forth the sun and moon and stars from out of nothing; admirable, when He divided the waters from the dry land, and covered the earth with green things, and peopled it with animals, and, lastly, brought forth man to be the Lord of all creation; admirable in His justice, when He let loose the waters of the earth, and, opening the floodgates of Heaven, utterly destroyed those, who were guilty, of the sons of men; admirable in His merciful dealings with the family of Abraham, with the race of Israel. But yet more admirable in the incarnation of His Son and the fruits of His glorious Redemption.

Often we are transported with joy in beholding the material beauties of God's creation; and we do well to admire and love His every work. But how much more delight ought we to find in the contemplation of the wonders of His grace. The body is worth more than the raiment, and moral beauty infinitely surpasses material or physical beauty. Now, what more perfect specimen of moral beauty could we find, than the regenerated soul of the Penitent

Thief? From a barren wilderness, it has been changed into a lovely, fruitful garden, rich with every virtue; fit, indeed, to find a place even in the Paradise of God. Ah! let us learn to love this great saint as he deserves; to imitate him henceforth in his holiness, as we have but too surely imitated him, hitherto, in his wickedness; and, in admiring the wonders of his miraculous conversion, we cannot fail to increase our love of Him Who worked it, Whose arm is not shortened and Whose mercy endureth for ever.

CHAPTER 20

The Good Thief's Claim to Martyrdom

WE have spoken of the soul of Dismas as of a most perfect specimen of moral beauty — a very master-piece. Surely, it is not possible that the most precious gem of all should be wanting to his crown; that gem, the price of which is greater, than the united value of the rest; a gem which is like the pearl brought from afar; or like that treasure of which the Gospel speaks, which, when he had found, the merchant went and for joy thereof, sold all his goods and bought it? I mean the glory of martyrdom — a glory so great that it raises the least of the faithful far above priests and missionaries, confessors and pontiffs, and even doctors of the Church. Some would have us believe that this glory, at least, is not to be found in our saint. We maintain that it is. Let us, however, critically examine the question.

According to the teaching of Catholic theology, martyrdom requires three conditions. First, that death be suffered, or such torments as would naturally cause death. Secondly, that the suffering should be voluntary. Thirdly, that it be borne in defence of the faith, or of some other of the Christian virtues. From these premises, many would be inclined to conclude that Dismas did not suffer martyrdom. And certainly, at first sight, it would seem that his sufferings were not voluntary, and that they were not borne in defence of faith or any other Christian virtue, but rather as the penalty for sin.

But Cyprian, the great martyr-saint of Carthage, answers these objections, in the following terms: "In the passion of this thief we have to consider two distinct periods — two men, as it were, and two sorts of blood. The blood shed before the advent of faith was the blood of a thief; but that shed afterwards, the blood of a Christian. The blood of the thief was but a guilt-stained sacrifice; but the blood of the Christian, shed in testimony of the faith — as a witness that Christ is truly the Son of God — that blood, was the blood of a confessor (i.e., martyr)."[1]

St. Augustine repeats and adopts the opinion of his illustrious colleague. "The thief who before was not a disciple of Christ, but became a confessor upon the cross, is numbered by the holy Cyprian among the martyrs... To have confessed Christ upon the cross, weighed as much in the scale of merit as if he had been crucified for Christ's sake. Thus we find the martyr's privilege in him, who believed in Christ, when the future martyrs had all fled away and left Him."[2]

In another place, the same great Doctor says: "The thief had not yet been called, and was already elect; not yet a servant, he became a friend; a master, without having served as disciple; one moment a thief, the next a confessor. So that although he began his sufferings as a robber, he ended them as a martyr."[3]

We find the same thought expressed by St. Jerome. In one of his letters to St. Paulinus he says: "The thief exchanged the cross for Paradise; and turned the penalty of murder into a glorious martyrdom."[4]

St. Hilary speaks of our Lord as "promising Paradise to this his martyr."[5]

And St. Bernard, thus: "O blessed thief — or rather, not so much thief as martyr and confessor — thou didst voluntarily accept what necessity had forced upon thee, and didst change chastisement into glory, and the cross into a triumph! In thee, most blessed confessor and martyr, Christ gathered what was left of faith, amid the general barrenness of the world. Thou on the cross didst take the place of Peter; and in the house of Caiphas, Peter played the thief. And this did he so long as, hiding what he really was, he outwardly denied his Divine Master. For which reason thou didst precede him into Paradise. For He Who received thee upon the cross having become thy chief and guide, took thee with Him; and, the same day of His entry into His Kingdom, He introduced there also His faithful and glorious soldier."[6]

The authorities I have quoted above are assuredly numerous and venerable enough to place beyond doubt our saint's title to martyrdom. But because they all found it upon this, that he suffered the torments of the cross — at least in part — in testimony to our Lord's Divinity, I will add a few words upon another suffering which, in the opinion of many, was inflicted upon him solely for that cause. I speak of the *crurifragium,* or breaking of the legs.

The torment of the *crurifragium* was quite distinct from that of crucifixion, and was not generally inflicted upon the same person. Of this we find many proofs in the records of history. Thus, Seneca, in speaking of the atrocities of Sylla, tells us that by his orders M. Marius Gratidianus had his legs broken, as well as his eyes put out, and his hands cut off.[7] And in Suetonius we read that: "Augustus having discovered that his secretary, Thallus, had received 500 pieces of silver in exchange for a letter that he had given up, ordered him to have his legs broken."[8]

The same writer tells us of another occasion upon which this punishment was inflicted; but this time under Tiberius, and not because of crime, but with an injustice, the circumstances of which are too horrible to relate."[9]

The torment of the *crurifragium* was by no means peculiar to the Romans. On the contrary, traces of it are found amongst almost all the peoples of antiquity. We will give but one instance, recorded by Polybius: "The Spendiani, African rebels, when they had taken prisoners the chief men of Carthage, broke their legs, and, otherwise horribly mutilating them, threw them, while still alive, into a pit."[10]

It is unnecessary to add that this torture was frequently made use of against the Christian martyrs. The Acts of the Martyrdom of St. Adrian, among many others, give an account of it, such as may serve to convey some idea both of the cruelty of the imperial tyrants, and of the glorious constancy of the confessors of the faith.

What we have said is, we think, sufficient to prove that the *crurifragium* had no necessary connection whatever with crucifixion. This latter torment was so terrible that it was not lightly put an end to by the infliction of another torture which was almost instantaneously fatal. The ancient law-givers were, on the contrary, anxious to prolong as much as possible the sufferings of those crucified, so that the lesson of terror should be more striking to onlookers, and consequently, as they thought, more efficacious. For their sufferings to be put an end to any sooner than usual it was necessary that there should be some grave reason — such as a public feastday, or the birthday of the ruling prince; sometimes, also, the prayer of their relations or friends, if they happened to be persons of consequence — otherwise those crucified were left hanging upon the cross until their bodies fell into corruption.[11]

With the Jews, as with the Gentiles, crucifixion and *crurifragium* were two entirely separate methods of inflicting death. In that passage of Deuteronomy which treats of crucifixion, not a word is said of any further punishment. On the contrary, that passage itself forms by its silence a negative proof that the *crurifragium* was not inflicted. Here is the text: "When a man hath committed a crime for which he is to be punished with death, and, being condemned to die, is hanged on a gibbet, his body shall not remain upon the tree, but shall be buried the same day, for he is accursed of God that hangeth on a tree: and thou shalt not defile thy land, which the Lord thy God shall give thee in possession." (Deut 21:22-23)

The breaking of the criminal's legs was therefore nowise ordered by the law, nor does it appear to have been authorized by any later custom. As to what took place on Calvary, let us listen to the Commentary of Origen, which is especially valuable on all these points of detail, its illustrious author having been so well versed in all the customs of the East. Living as he did in the times of persecution, it is needless to say that he was thoroughly acquainted with every form of capital punishment. On the words of St. John — "Then the Jews (because it was the Parasceve), that the bodies might not remain upon the cross on the Sabbath day (for that was a great Sabbath day), besought Pilate that their legs might be broken, and that they might be taken away;"(Jn 20:31) — on these words, the great commentator remarks: "These things were done at the time of Christ's condemnation. That Pilate, in commanding that the body of Christ should be broken, was not acting in accordance with the usual custom, seems evident from the very wording of the text; (they) besought Pilate that their legs might be broken, and that they might be taken away. Would it have been necessary to pray and beseech him for leave to do this if it must have been done in the ordinary course?"[12]

Now there were, as we have already said, certain cases in which the Romans allowed the bodies to be taken down from the cross before the ordinary time, and we can well understand that the great paschal feast of the Jews should have been thought sufficient reason to warrant this unusual procedure. But in these cases death was generally hastened, not by breaking the legs of the criminal, but by piercing his heart with a lance. That Pilate had given no such order in regard to our Lord was probably, as Origen suggests, owing to his desire of conciliating the Jews.[13] For which reason, also, he allowed the *crurifragium* at their request, and hence his wonder on hearing that Christ was already dead. He knew that those crucified lingered on for hours, and even days, and therefore he hesitated to allow Joseph of Arimathea to take down the Lord's body, until he had learnt the truth from the centurion.

The providence of God overruled the order obtained from Pilate for breaking the legs of our Lord, as says the Evangelist: "that the Scripture might be fulfilled, *Ye shall not break a bone of Him*" (Jn 9:36; Ex 12:43; Num 9:12) The same mysterious counsel, foretold in prophecy, explains the reason why the Savior's side was pierced by the lance. We may also, in part, attribute this last blow to the custom which obtained of thus killing those who were taken down from the cross on the very day of their crucifixion. But this custom, the reason of which was to ensure death, was not in itself sufficient motive for the blow, seeing that our Lord was already dead, when He received it.

A trace of this custom long survived in the criminal code of Europe. During the Middle Ages (and in some countries almost down to our own time) to break a criminal upon the wheel was not an uncommon punishment, but generally the executioner began by giving him a blow somewhere near the heart, which had the effect of making him almost, if not quite, unconscious of the agony caused by the instrument of torture. But in some cases, where the criminal was more than ordinarily guilty, the blow upon the heart was only given as the finishing stroke. To this custom, we owe the term *coup de grace,* which is so often used without any notion of its penal origin.

The question remains, Why did the Jews, in asking to have the bodies taken down from the cross, also pray that their legs might be broken, instead of allowing death to be inflicted in the usual and more merciful way, by means of the lance? The answer is easily found in their blind hatred of our Lord, and also, perhaps, not less in their furious rage at the boldness with which Dismas had proclaimed His innocence and their consequent guilt. When Pilate had written the Savior's title — King of the Jews — they had done their utmost to persuade him to change it, but in vain. They were angry, but had no means of expressing their anger. But when one of the thieves dared to acknowledge the Kingly character of their Victim, and by his words to make it known to all the people, then, indeed, was their wrath tenfold enkindled, and they determined to be revenged. Therefore they went into Pilate and "besought that their legs might be broken." The blasphemies of the bad thief might well have exempted him from further punishment at their hands, but they could not do any different to him without further explanation to Pilate and from this they shrank. Besides, with men so lost to truth, so utterly carried away by their passions, one injustice more would seem but a small thing.

That revenge was the intention of the Jews in asking for the *crurifragium,* seems to have been the general opinion of the fathers. Commenting on the words of St. John — *"The soldiers therefore came, and they broke the legs of the first and of the other that was crucified with Him* — Luke of Burgos says: "The first was the thief who was crucified on the right hand, and who had been justified through the blood of Christ."[14]

"To what purpose these minute details?" asks St. Gregory. "Is it possible for us to believe that they were given, as it were, accidentally, without some deep meaning. If so, it would have been simpler to state merely that they broke the legs of the two thieves. But in the words, "They broke the legs of the *first and of the other* is hidden a mysterious sense."[15]

This sense is given us by the learned Padre Sylveira, on the authority of Euthymius: "By the first is signified the thief crucified on the right hand, and purified in the Blood of Christ. As the just is ever the first to endure torments, so they began by breaking the legs of the converted thief, because of the hate they felt towards one who was a confessor of Christ."[16]

Whence the same writer concludes that Dismas was truly a martyr, and that the fathers of the Church were fully justified in giving him this glorious title. "First they broke the legs of this blessed thief, and that with great rage and fury. Wherefore, as Dismas patiently suffered this on account of the sublime testimony he had given to the innocence and kingship of Christ, I do not hesitate to speak of him as a martyr, in common with the holy fathers."[17]

Nevertheless, historic truth compels me to admit that there have always been two opinions on the subject of St. Dismas' claim to the martyr's crown. In the last century the question was brought before the Congregation of Rites. Their decision is characteristic of the extreme prudence observed at Rome in relation to all doubtful matters. Without in the slightest degree blaming, or even disapproving, the opinion of those fathers and doctors of the Church who give to our saint the title of martyr, the Sacred Congregation decided that the title was not to be inserted in the liturgy, and that the office of the Good Thief was to be that of a *Confessor non Pontifex;* and, to avoid all possibility of cavil or criticism, the traditional name of Dismas was also omitted.

CHAPTER 21

The Good Thief's Reward

WE have already seen that Dismas did all, and more than all, which is required of a repentant sinner. He had examined his past life, and had confessed his sins with the deepest sorrow, and, humbly and lovingly, he had turned his heart towards God. He had done this with great earnestness and sincerity, and with heroic courage. And so, all barriers being done away with, the grace of God entered into and flooded his soul, even as the light of day pours into a dark room, when once the windows thereof are opened.

Nay, more, the divine Mercy received the thief as a mother would receive a long-lost child, as the father of the prodigal received his son.

My words are all too weak to be able fittingly to paint this mystery of love and forgiveness. What shall I say, what analogy shall I find, in anywise to express it? Let us take the case of a criminal condemned to death. Alone, bound in chains, he awaits his last hour at the bottom of some noisome dungeon. His whole life passes before him in review — a procession of grisly phantoms, not a thing which gives him comfort. His execution is not yet begun; but already he is tormented by a twofold agony — remorse for the past, fear for the future. At last the jailer appears and leads him forth and gives him over to the minister of justice, at whose hands he is to receive the penalty of death. But if, on his way to execution, this unhappy wretch were to meet his king, and be forgiven his crimes, and have his sentence remitted, what words could tell his joy and gratitude?

A thousand-fold greater must have been the happiness of Dismas when he heard from our Lord the gracious promise: "This day shalt thou be with Me in Paradise." Let us weigh well the sense of those divine words, that we may understand, to some extent at least, the joy they produced in him to whom they were addressed. The thief heard in them the certainty of pardon, grace, and everlasting glory. How much was included in that single word pardon! His whole life had been one long sin. He had grown old in wickedness, and had been condemned of God, and hated and loathed by all his fellow men. And now, in a moment, he was rescued from the jaws of hell, forgiven all his sins, cleansed from every stain, freed from the pangs of remorse and shame. With these words of pardon, the sweet healing balm of peace was poured into his wounded soul, and joy, such as he had never felt before or even dreamt of.

The Good Thief was pardoned. But might he not be troubled with the thought of, perhaps, forfeiting his pardon? Might he not fear to fall again into the abyss out of which he had just been rescued? But no! The words of the Savior left no room for doubt or fear. With an oath, He had confirmed them. No more falling away was possible for Dismas. That very day, he was to enter Paradise.

In truth, nothing could be stronger than the words used by our Lord. The word Amen (so be it) is never made use of in Scripture, except upon the most solemn occasions.[1] Here, it conveyed to Dismas the certainty of his salvation, by assuring him of the grace of perseverance, even unto death.[2] But, as though this one word were not enough, our Lord deigns to repeat it. As says St. Ambrose: "The Gospel shows clearly that the word Amen is the highest asseveration ever made use of by our Lord to confirm His prophecies and promises. It has even greater force where it is repeated, as it is written, 'Amen, Amen, I say to thee, this day shalt thou be with Me in Paradise.'"[3]

Through these words not only did Dismas obtain the pardon of his past life, and the gracious assurance of his future perseverance in good, but also the promise of an immediate entry into the glory of his Lord. That very day he was to enter into Life, into joys untold, into happiness without end. It is indeed impossible for us to say what must have been the intensity of his grateful love toward Christ in the midst of this torrent of heavenly delight.

One thing, at least, we may safely say — that his supernatural happiness was so great as to make him utterly forgetful of all physical pain; so that, to use the words of one of his chief panegyrists: "The thought of his agony was washed away by the overflowing of his great love."[4] Like that other illustrious convert, St. Paul, Dismas was able to say in truth: "I exceedingly abound with joy in all tribulations." (2 Cor 7:4)

Forerunner of the martyrs, the Good Thief experienced upon the cross what they also felt amid their sufferings. He likewise might have said: "Never have I assisted at so glorious a feast."[5] But this joy amid tribulation, great as it was, was not all the Savior promised to His beloved confessor. He held out to him a happiness which should be perfect and unmixed; and this, not at some future, distant time, but at once, that very day. The fathers of the Church cannot contain their admiration at the treasures of tenderness and love contained in these life-giving words. Let us hearken to St. Augustine as the spokesman of them all.

"The Good Thief had said: 'Remember me,' not now, but 'when Thou shalt come into Thy kingdom. I have sinned too deeply to be worthy of immediate happiness. This would be too much; let me suffer yet awhile, at least until Thine entry into glory. Do Thou forgive me then.' Thus the thief strove to put off his reward. But the Lord would not have it so. That very day, He bade him enter into the joys of Paradise."[6]

"See what loving kindness!" exclaims a contemporary of St. Bernard's. "He does not merely say, 'Thou shalt be in Paradise,' or 'Thou shalt be with the angels;' but 'Thou shalt be with Me!'"[7] Yea, thou shalt see, in the glory of His Majesty, Him Whom thou hast so nobly confessed in His infirmity. Thou hast suffered with Me on the cross, now shalt thou share with Me the delights of My kingdom. Neither shalt thou have long to wait for thy reward. This day shalt thou enjoy it. "Such is the goodness of our sweet Savior that, without delay, He hears and answers prayer. He promises, and at once He gives."[8] Who then, I ask, shall dare to doubt His love? Who shall despair of forgiveness? Ay, we also have tasted the sweetness of Thy name, and our hope shall not be confounded, for never dost Thou abandon those who put their trust in Thee!

Such was the eagerness of our Lord — if we may so speak — to introduce the thief into His Kingdom, that for this purpose, He set aside all the ordinary rules of His governance. He had previously appointed Peter the doorkeeper of the Heavenly Jerusalem; but on this occasion the King, Himself, deigned to unlock the gates and bring into the city His faithful companion. Arnold of Chartres develops this somewhat quaint idea, at considerable length, in the following passage. Addressing himself to St. Peter, he says:

"Be not angry, O thou, prince of the Apostles and doorkeeper of Heaven. I see thee not at the foot of the cross; fear keeps thee hidden: thou hast not even the courage to accompany the Mother of thy Master, and the holy women who follow her to the foot of the Cross. Thou makest no use of thine apostolic power of binding and loosing. Thou art absent whilst the Savior and the sinner are speaking together. Forgive me, if I say that thou neglectest thy porter's office. The Supreme High Priest supplies thy place, and unbolts the ancient bars. The Lord, Himself, brings into His Kingdom the thief, who, as the first-fruits of those despaired of, He places upon the throne of the rebel Lucifer. And he whom thou, perhaps, wouldst not have forgiven seven times, albeit guilty of offences seventy times seven repeated, is absolved by the good Jesus, and reigns henceforth amid the angels of God.

"Oh, take back thine office and learn to forgive. Look neither to the number nor the heinousness of sins confessed.

The mercy of God knows no bounds. It is not hedged in by numbers, nor limited by time. If any ask, to him shall be given. Whoso repenteth, findeth pardon. Note well the lesson. It is the eleventh, the last hour; the man forgiven is the chief of sinners. His iniquities are countless, their guilt exceeding great, but, in a moment, all is washed away by the grace of God — by the baptism of His mercy is this poor soul made clean.

"What an example, this, of the Good Thief! He repents, and at once he becomes to us a model of penance and a cause of hope. He seeks and finds — he asks and immediately he receives. Where shall we find a more wonderful instance of the action of God's mercy, or one more perfect and complete? The thief is spared the expiatory flames. He goes straight to Heaven, to make known our pardon, himself the witness and the first-fruit of our redemption, and he makes his triumphal entry amid the songs and canticles of the angelic host: 'This day shalt thou be with me in Paradise.'"[9]

There are mysteries hidden in every smallest detail of the Passion of our Blessed Lord; and the holy doctors, in studying it by the help of tradition, have continually discovered therein fresh lights and harmonies ever new. In following their pious investigations step by step we now come to this question: At what hour did Christ promise Paradise to the Good Thief? The fathers all make answer that it was at the hour of noon. And for this reason, that, at that same hour, Adam had been driven out of Paradise, and the gates thereof shut; until the time when, by the death of the new Adam, the eternal gates should be lifted up, and the King of Glory should enter in, bringing with Him the penitent thief as the first-fruits of them whom He had died to save. It was fitting, therefore, that the words of peace and reconciliation should be spoken by the Savior at the same hour in which the former sentence had been carried out — the sentence of wrath and punishment. Hence it is that the hour of noon has always been considered among Christians as an hour specially sacred and holy.[10]

Let us stop to gather up a few gleanings of the patristic teaching on this point. The one great, all-sufficing reason of the

Church's having consecrated to prayer the hour of noon is to be found in this, that at that hour our Lord was lifted up upon the Cross. At that hour also, Adam was created, it being the sixth hour of the sixth day. Noon was the time at which sin entered the world; whence the same hour was chosen for the Reparation, which had been marked by the Fall. At noon, likewise, it was that God foretold to Abraham the birth of his son, from whom was to come the Desired of Nations. Already, at the time of the covenant of circumcision, God had made known the promise to His servant; but under the tree in the valley of Mambre, in the mid-day heat, it was that the promise was renewed, and heard by Sara, who laughed, but presently believed. At noon, Joseph, the type and figure of our Lord, was let down into the pit. At the same hour it was that he feasted his brethren in Egypt. At noon, Ruth was gleaning in the field of Boaz, when her lord came near and spoke to her, and provided food for her nourishment, even as Christ feedeth His spouse, the Church. It was about the sixth hour, too, when our Lord received the Gentiles in the person of the Samaritan woman, to whom He gave to drink of the living water, as He sat by Jacob's Well.

And finally at noon, the sixth hour of the sixth day of the sixth week of the sixth period of the world's history, we find the realization of all these types and figures in the Redeemer Who at that hour was lifted up upon the Cross, through which He was to save mankind. On the sixth day, God had rested from the work of creation. At the sixth hour and day His only begotten Son likewise completed His great work — the work of our Redemption.

Now we come to a further question: What was that Paradise of which our Lord promised immediate possession to the Good Thief? It was certainly not that place which we generally mean when we speak of Heaven; for we know that our Savior Himself did not go up there until forty days after His resurrection. But the Heavenly Paradise is not solely the abode of the just made perfect. It is not so much a place as a state. He dwells in Heaven, to whom it is given to enjoy the Beatific Vision. Our Lord promised Dismas that he should be with Him, that day in Paradise. The being with Him was what, in itself, constituted Paradise. Hence, we may infer that the soul of the Good Thief accompanied our Lord in His descent into Limbo.

"We shall be the better able to understand the sense (of these words of our Lord)" . . . says St. Augustine, "if we take them as having been spoken by Christ, as God, rather than as man. . . . As man, Christ was to be that day in the tomb, as regarded His body, and in hell, as regarded His soul: but as God, Christ is always everywhere. . . . Wheresoever Paradise may be, all the Blessed are there, when they are together with Him Who is everywhere."[11]

St.Thomas speaks in the same sense: "Christ, by going straightways down to hell, set free the saints who were detained there; not, however, by at once leading them out of the place of hell, but by making the light of His glory to shine upon them, even in hell itself. For so it was fitting that His soul should abide in hell, so long as His body was left in the grave. That word of the Lord ('This day shalt thou be with me in Paradise') must therefore be understood not of an earthly or corporeal Paradise, but of that spiritual paradise in which all may be, said to be, who are in the enjoyment of the Divine Glory. Hence, as to place, the thief went down with Christ into hell, that he might be with Christ, as it was said to him: 'Thou shalt be with Me in Paradise;' but as to reward, he was in Paradise, for he there tasted and enjoyed the divinity of Christ, together with the other saints."

Was the Good Thief the first to be admitted to the delights of the Beatific Vision, before all the ancient patriarchs and prophets who so long had been waiting the coming of the Messiah? That this was the case seems to be the opinion of many of the fathers. St. Chrysostom, speaking of Dismas, says: "Our Lord was not ashamed that he should be the first to enter Paradise."[12] St. Augustine, St. Eulogius, and others speak in like manner.[13]

If we take the words of these great doctors in their literal sense, we may conclude therefrom, that the Good Thief was given the enjoyment of the Beatific Vision from the very moment, when our Lord said to him the words: This day, shalt thou be with me in Paradise; for otherwise he would not have been the first — for we know that our Lord died before Dismas, and that his soul went down to Limbo, bringing with it the joys of Heaven to those who were there already. However this may be, we may say without doubt or hesitation that, from the first moment of his death, the Good Thief came into everlasting possession of happiness far surpassing all that the human heart could wish for, of beauty, of sweetness, and of glory; delights such as eye hath not seen, nor ear heard, nor hath it entered into the mind of man to conceive.

CHAPTER 22

The Good Thief's Reward (continued)

THE happiness of the saints, whose souls are now in Heaven, is doubtless perfect and without alloy. Nevertheless, it is not boundless, and consequently is susceptible of increase. I do not here speak of that which is termed by theologians accidental glory; but of that increase of happiness which will be given to the elect at the general resurrection, when, by the reunion of soul and body, man shall be restored to the primeval perfection of his being, such as it came forth from the hands of God. In the words of the great St. Thomas: "It may in truth be said that after the resurrection, the happiness of the saints will be very considerably increased, because then their happiness will no longer be confined to the soul, but enjoyed by the body, also. And it may even be said that the happiness of the soul itself will be greatly added to, inasmuch as the soul will then rejoice not only in its own good, but in that, moreover, of the body." Reason joyfully accepts this teaching, which satisfies one of the strongest natural cravings of the human heart.

In a few rare instances, that law has been dispensed with which ordains that after death the bodies, even of the elect, should be left here below, waiting the great regeneration of all things. No Catholic doubts but what this was the case with the pure and holy body of the Mother of God. Some, however, are inclined to believe that this privilege was also conferred upon several others, and notably upon the Good Thief. Let us now examine whether there are sufficient grounds for holding this opinion.

We read in the Gospel: "And Jesus again crying out with a loud voice, yielded up the ghost. And behold the veil of the Temple was rent in twain from the top even to the bottom, and the earth quaked, and the rocks were rent. And the graves were opened, and many bodies of the saints that had slept arose, and coming out of the tombs after His resurrection, came into the Holy City and appeared to many." (Mt 27:50-53)

All these prodigies were the result and consequence of that surpassing great wonder, the death of the Man-God. The veil of the Temple was rent in twain to show that the Mosaic dispensation had reached its end. Nature, struck with horror and shame, gave trembling witness to her Creator's death by the rending of the rocks, by the earthquake, and by the universal darkness in which she shrouded her grief. In this we have also a figure of the general convulsion which will precede the final judgment, when the earth shall be moved, and the heavens depart, with a great noise. One of the thieves repented and was forgiven, the other blasphemed and was condemned. Herein we read the doom of man. Free choice is given him, but, once made, it is irrevocable. Happy they who choose as Dismas chose! The graves were opened, and death gave up its spoils, as proof of the redemption of Christ and pledge of the great resurrection to come.

It is not our purpose to enter into a study of each one of these miracles. The raising up of the dead alone concerns our subject. We have, therefore, to examine who those saints were, whose bodies arose; to whom they showed themselves; the time of their resurrection; and what afterwards became of their bodies, when their souls went up to Heaven.

It is certain that our Lord was the first to rise again; for which reason St. John speaks of Him as "the firstborn of the dead," (Apoc 1-5) and St. Paul as "the first-fruits of them that sleep."(1 Cor 15:20) Moreover, the sacred text itself states clearly that the bodies of the saints came "out of the tombs *after* His resurrection." (Mt 27:50-53) These saints indeed arose, as says

St. Jerome, that they might bear witness to their risen Lord.[1] Obviously, therefore, His resurrection must have taken place before theirs, else it could not have derived therefrom any corroborative proof.

All the wonders spoken of by St. Matthew, in the afore-quoted text, were done within a short time of Christ's death; but not all the same day, as his words themselves show. He classes them all together to avoid having to come back to the same subject, which would interfere with the rapid concentrated nature of his history. According to Suarez, that miracle which was the greatest of all, was partly worked on the day of our Lord's death, partly on that of His resurrection. The graves were opened at the general rending of the rocks on Good Friday, but the bodies arose only on Easter morning. "For so," concludes this great mystical writer, "had Divine Providence ordained, that their resurrection should be made more clearly evident, from the fact of their having been seen so lately lying dead in the opened tombs."[2]

When, therefore, the new Adam had come forth triumphant from the grave, having put to flight death and hell, numbers of those whom He had raised came into the Holy City, and announced to many the glorious tidings of His redemption. How eloquently must they have preached to them faith and repentance. Their very appearance in itself was sufficient argument to convince the most hardened, and to their influence may, perhaps, be, in part, attributed, the great number of those who believed in the words of Peter on the Day of Pentecost. For forty days, they had been convinced of their sin in rejecting the Messias. In fear and trembling they had wondered what they were to do to escape the coming judgment; and gladly they accepted the means offered them by the Apostles.

The Holy Gospel tells us that those who arose were many, and that they appeared unto many, but it does not tell us who they were, or whether our saint was of the number. To ascertain this we must have recourse to tradition, which supplies evidence of so much which is left unrecorded in Scripture. The fathers of the Church tell us that those arose who were more specially connected with our Lord, either by the bonds of the flesh or of prophecy.[3] Thus our first parents, and the patriarchs and prophets. To these the types and figures of Christ were added; also, the just men who had died during His own lifetime; such as Zacharias, and John the Baptist, and Simeon, and St. Joseph, and many others, among whom, also, the Good Thief.[4] St. Epiphanius, who was so well versed in all the traditions of the East, specially insists upon the resurrection of these last,[5] and for a reason which we can easily understand. All the elements and powers of Nature had borne witness to the divinity of the Lamb sacrificed upon Calvary. Their witness was strong, clear, and unmistakable. But when the very dead were raised up for the same purpose, it was not possible that their witness should be less distinct.

For this, it was not enough for the ancients alone to give testimony; there were no means of verifying their credentials, so to speak. Men could not recognize Adam, or Abraham, or Moses, or Jeremiah, whom they had never seen; but not so with Zacharias, or Simeon, or Dismas, who had been known to all the people. When these appeared to their friends and kinsmen, and allowed them to touch them, and to prove to themselves that they were not phantoms but the real bodies of those who had slept, there was no longer room for doubt. And these would vouch for the identity of those other, greater dead, the awe of whose presence would then be felt in all its strength, and their message received with the respect due to their high authority.

Now, are we to suppose that these glorious witnesses re-assumed their bodies only temporarily, and that, after having appeared to many in the Holy City, they underwent a second death, being once more separated from them? Such a notion seems to me highly improbable, and it is, moreover, contrary to the opinion of our best theologians. They hold that the risen saints remained upon the earth until the day of our Lord's ascension; and that, like Him, they appeared frequently during that time unto those who were worthy to see them — *testibus*

prœordinatis, in scholastic phrase — confirming them more and
more in their faith, and preparing them for the work they had
to do, in tending of the infant Church. Finally, on Ascension
Day, they were taken up, body and soul, with Christ into Heaven,
and shown forth to His Almighty Father and the angelic host
as the glorious trophies of His victory over sin and death, and
the perfect first-fruits of the regenerated human race.

Among those theologians who hold this beautiful and consoling opinion we will cite only these: Venerable Bede, St. Anselm,
Rabanus Maurrus, Paschasius Radbert, Druthmar, Rupert, Cajetan,
Jansenius, Dionysius of Chartres, Maldonatus, Cornelius à Lapide,
and the great Suarez.[6]

If the authority of these great writers is not enough, we
can refer to the early fathers, on whose opinion theirs is built
up. Among others, St. Epiphanius, speaking of relics, says: "The
relics of all the saints are upon the earth, except of those who
rose again and showed themselves in the Holy City."[7] And
St. Sophronius, Patriarch of Jerusalem, in his synodal letter, recorded
and approved by the Sixth General Council, speaks thus: "On
the third day Christ rose again from the grave, and came forth,
bringing with Him all the dead whom He had raised from their
tombs, leading them from corruption to immortality by the power
of His own resurrection from the dead." (Act. 11.)

The earlier witness of Eusebius is even more clear and
definite. Speaking of our Lord's resurrection, he says: "His dead
body being raised to life, many bodies also of the saints, who
had slept, arose and went in with Him into the holy, even the
true, Heavenly City."[8] So well grounded did this opinion appear
to St. Anselm, and, indeed, so generally accepted, that he does
not hesitate to say that "no credence is to be given to the unfounded
assertions of those who rashly maintain that (the bodies of the
saints who arose) afterwards returned into dust." (In Mt 27:53)

Of the resurrection of Dismas in particular the learned
Raynaldus speaks in the following terms: "It was fitting that
Christ should have, in the integrity of His human nature, him,
who had shared His Cross and passion, as the companion of

His resurrection and happiness. Thus the thief may be said to be, wholly and entirely, with the undivided Christ; not so, merely in part. We may add to this that nowhere are to be found the smallest relics of the Good Thief. It is not likely that Christ would suffer so great a treasure to remain forever hidden in the earth, if it were really to be found there."[9]

In conclusion, we may safely say, with the great Archbishop of Rheims, St. Remi, who had thoroughly sifted the whole question, that reason and tradition alike "force us to believe that those who, at the Lord's resurrection, rose again from the dead, also, when He ascended into Heaven, were taken up thither together with Him."[10]

Was it not, indeed, to be expected that Christ should take with Him in His triumph those whom, by His death, He had set free? Such souls, having been stamped with the glorious seal of immortality, could not surely, even for a moment, be united to corruptible bodies, and thus exposed to suffer from heat and cold and any other natural causes; to be subject to every human infirmity, and finally, to death. If these saints were to be condemned to a second death, far better would it have been for them, not to have been raised from the dead. Yet we know, from the Gospel, that they were in truth united to their natural bodies; whence we cannot fail to infer that those bodies had received the attributes of immortality. And can we suppose that glorified bodies should return to dust and corruption? Far more easy is it to believe, with so many of the fathers and doctors of the Church, that the bodies which arose, and were seen in the Holy City, were afterwards translated, together with the souls to which they had been reunited, to the kingdom of Heaven. Thus, and thus alone, could these saints be shown forth by Christ as complete and perfect specimens of the fruits of His redemption; for a disembodied spirit, though glorified, is not a perfect man.

From all which, we will boldly conclude, with Suarez and Cornelius à Lapide, that of all opinions on this subject, that which places the bodies of the saints who arose on Easter Day together with their souls in Paradise, is the most reasonable, the most true, the best grounded upon authority and tradition; and, being in strict keeping with the natural instincts, is also the best fitted to show forth, in their true light, the divine mercy, and love, and glory of the risen Christ.[11]

Among these illustrious companions of His glory there is one whom our Lord will ever look upon with an especial love and joy. I allude to St. Dismas, the converted thief. Let us listen to better words than mine, the words of the great St. Chrysostom:

"What king is there, who, entering in triumph into his capital, would make to sit down by his side a highway robber, or even any one of his servants? Yet this is what our Lord deigned to do when entering His heavenly home — He brought with Him the thief. But this was not a disgrace to Paradise, but a glory, rather.

"The glory of Paradise is to have a King so powerful, as to be able to make a thief worthy to share in its delights. In the same way, when He brought publicans and sinners into the Heavenly Kingdom, He did not detract from, but rather increased the glory of Paradise. For by so doing He showed clearly His divine power, which can easily make even publicans and sinners holy enough to be really fit for such grace and happiness.

"As we admire a physician most when we see him healing what seemed to be incurable wounds, and restoring to health those sick unto death, so it is right that we should specially admire our blessed Lord when we see Him, healing the incurable, and bringing back publicans, and sinful women, to such a perfect state of moral health as to be fit to reign with the angels in Heaven.

"Would ye ask what this thief has done to deserve to be taken straight from the cross to Heaven? I will make answer in these two words: whilst Peter was below, denying (Christ), he was confessing Him on high! Do not therefore, I pray you, forget this Good Thief; and let us not be ashamed to receive as our teacher, one whom our Lord was not ashamed to bring, the first, into Paradise."[12]

CHAPTER 23

The Glory of the Good Thief

S T. PAUL, speaking of charity, calls it "the bond of perfection." This expression is as profoundly true as it is beautiful.
God, indeed, is the Center and End of all perfection, "God
is love," as says St. John. The love, which unites man to God,
is therefore the most sacred link, the very bond of perfection. And
the more the bond is tightly, closely drawn, the greater man's
perfection. Hence we may say that during this earthly life, the value
and merit of every virtue is derived from charity, and may be
measured thereupon.

St. Augustine goes further, and defines charity, not only
as the greatest of all virtues, but as the essence of each. "Whereas
it is virtue which leads us to a life of bliss: I affirm that virtue
is naught else but the supreme love of God. The several virtues
are but various forms and manifestations of charity, and I do
not hesitate to define them as follows: Faith is love that believes;
Hope, love that waits and trusts; Patience, suffering love; Prudence, wisely-discerning love; Justice, the love that renders to
each one the things that are due; Fortitude, a bold love, strong
to act; Temperance, a jealous love, reserving itself wholly for
its beloved."[1]

Now, if on earth, charity is the measure of the perfection
of saints, so, in Heaven, it is the measure of their reward. We
have already seen that Dismas was possessed of love in a heroic

degree; consequently his faith, and hope, and patience, and prudence, justice, fortitude, and temperance, were all heroic too.
This we have also seen, at some length, already. Let us add
that his charity was exercised amid altogether exceptional
circumstances, through which he has earned for himself five
special privileges, which are not shared by any other of the saints
in Heaven.

Alone among all the inhabitants of the City of God,
St. Dismas will, to all eternity, enjoy the glory of having been:
first, the true and faithful copy of Christ crucified; second,
the advocate of the Son of God; third, the only being who
preached forth His divinity on Calvary; fourth, the comforter
of the Blessed Virgin in her sorrows; and, fifth, the type and
figure of the elect.

First. St. Dismas was the true and faithful copy of Christ crucified.
Men are proud of being thought to resemble some fine type of physical
or moral beauty. If they have special, unearthly gifts, we sometimes
speak of them as angelic or seraphic. But how great a prerogative
it is for a man to be God-like, even in the slightest degree. Be not
scandalized, if I claim such a prerogative for the Good Thief. You
will perhaps be inclined to say: "What has Christ to do with Belial?
and what likeness is there between the Sun of Justice and a sinner
stained with every crime? — between the spotless purity of the Lamb
of God and the dense spiritual darkness of the thief, a darkness yet
more dark than that physical darkness, which shrouded Calvary?"

The objection would be unanswerable if applied to Dismas,
such as he was when first nailed to the cross. But, you have
read this book in vain, if you have not understood that Dismas,
at the hour of his death, had become another man. As fire purifies
gold and frees it from all alloy and dross, and as the waters
of baptism cleanse the soul of a child and clothe it with beauty
untold, so the grace of God cleansed and purified the soul of
this thief, and made it well-pleasing, and holy in the sight of
its Maker and of His angels.

I do not say that none of the saints equaled Dismas in
holiness, but, I do say, that he alone was chosen to have a full

and perfect resemblance to Christ in the mode, the time, and the place of His death. No other saint died on Calvary; none other was the fellow sufferer of our Lord on the day of His sacred Passion.[2]

But if the outward likeness alone is what distinguishes Dismas from his compeers in holiness, the inner likeness is not for that less perfect — indeed, this it is which gives value to what would, otherwise, have been mere outward seeming. But for this, Dismas had been without merit, like the other, unrepentant thief. After his conversion he became a living member of Jesus Christ; like his Head he suffered death in expiation of sin. Christ, though innocent, bore on Him the iniquities of us all, and His death was the price of our forgiveness. The death of Dismas was also a sin-offering, expiatory, if not voluntary; the penalty indeed of his crimes, but also, so to speak, the fine accepted in lieu of eternal punishment.[3]

In becoming a member of the mystical body of Christ, Dismas was also admitted to the Communion of Saints, and thenceforth his merits were no longer merely personal; so that he might in very truth rejoice in his sufferings, and say with St. Paul: "I fill up those things that are wanting of the sufferings of Christ in my flesh for His body, which is the Church." (Colos. I. 24) If therefore, according to the same Apostle, every baptized Christian bears within him the likeness of Christ, how much more striking and perfect is this likeness in the Good Thief, who was baptized in his own blood at the side of our Divine Redeemer, at the same time as He Himself underwent His baptism of blood.

Second. St. Dismas was the advocate or defender of the Son of God. On the day when the King of Heaven and earth was condemned to death, the city of Jerusalem contained about a million men, its usual number of inhabitants having been enormously swollen by the strangers who flocked thither from all parts of the earth to celebrate the Paschal feasts. In relation to our Lord the multitude was divided into two camps — the camp of the enemies of the Nazarean, and that of His friends.

While Jesus was being buffeted, and spat upon, and dragged about through the streets of Jerusalem, from Caiphas to Pilate, from Pilate to Herod, and from Herod back again to Pilate, His enemies ceased not their cries of hate and rage, their accusations and false testimonies. But among His friends there reigned absolute silence, unless, perhaps, when broken by the oaths and denials of His chief disciple. When Pilate brought Him forth and showed Him to the people, bearing the crown of thorns and the purple garment, bruised and bleeding from head to foot, his enemies rent the air with shouts and cries of death, "Crucify Him! crucify Him!" But among his friends, the silence was still unbroken.

The same thing continued when He went forth to Calvary, bearing His own cross upon His bleeding shoulders. And, when at last, He was lifted up upon the tree of shame, louder still rose the jeers, and taunts, and insults, and revilings, and blasphemies with which His enemies triumphed over Him, in the hour of the Prince of Darkness. But, among His friends, not a voice was raised in His defence. And, yet, was there ever a more glorious cause to plead? Ah! if only they could have obtained leave to do it, what millions of angels would have come down from Heaven, swift as lightning, brighter than the sun, and with fervid eloquence have put His enemies to shame by revealing His divinity, His almighty power, and, above all, His boundless love for men, the true cause of the shame and suffering and death, which He had freely taken upon Himself for their salvation. But no, this great privilege was denied the angels; the Apostles dared not claim it; and it fell to the lot of the worst of sinners, even Dismas, the thief. Wonderful indeed that such a one should be chosen to exercise a prerogative, the greatness of which the human mind can hardly grasp!

Calmly and boldly our saint rebuked the enemies of Christ, and in a few short words proclaimed His innocence, and their guilt. Sublime, indeed, was his courage — sublime the strength of his brief defence: "This man hath done no evil!"

If we consider the circumstances of time and place in which this defence was made, and the position in which the advocate stood, who thus fearlessly braved the wrath of a people drunk with blood and fury; we shall, perhaps, be enabled in some sort to understand the glory of being singled out for so splendid a mission. Ah! would that we could also to some extent realize what must have been the gratitude of the dying Savior toward the one man, who defended and consoled Him in His agony, when all others had fled away.

In order to gain some faint idea of the relation of Dismas in regard to our Lord, let us take, as in a parable, the case of some earthly king who should have been torn from his throne, divested of his royal robes, and brought to judgment before some mock tribunal, and unjustly condemned to death. What would have been his feelings, if, at the last moment, when the defection and flight of his most favored courtiers and vassals had taken from him what little hope had remained after the treachery and denial of his most devoted adherents; what would have been his feelings, I say, if then, one of his meanest subjects, one who had lived in rebellion so long as his king was on the throne, had then come forward, and publicly done him homage, asking pardon for his past offences and proclaiming the injustice of his king's sentence and the infamy of his judges and causing them to draw back and tremble before the guilt of regicide. But, if it should chance that this king should regain his kingdom or if he were to establish his throne elsewhere, it is not difficult to imagine the many proofs by which he would show his gratitude to the one subject who had taken his part in his hour of need. He would load him with honors and riches, and would give heed to his advice and be careful to satisfy his every desire. All the inhabitants of his kingdom would honor and respect one who was worthy of so much admiration, and, bowing before him, the chief nobles would salute him as the defender of their king; all would seek his favor and friendship, and his influence would be the dominant one at court. Now if we double or quadruple, or, indeed, multiply an hundredfold, the love and gratitude which our supposed king would feel and show towards his advocate, we shall hardly obtain even a dim notion of the love and gratitude which our Lord shows to Dismas, now that He has made him to reign with Him in His everlasting Kingdom.

"Give me," says St. Chrysostom, "a thousand servants, who are faithful to their lord, whilst he is prosperous and honored of men, and one only servant who in the time of temptation follows his lord into suffering and exile, while the other thousand desert and leave him; and I ask you: shall these time-serving men be as well considered as him who stayed by his lord throughout? No, assuredly no. O ye patriarchs, prophets, apostles, evangelists, and martyrs, ye have cleaved to the Lord because ye did see Him in the majesty of His glory, doing great signs and wonders: but the Good Thief saw Him in His shame alone; yet nevertheless he followed Him, faithfully unto death."[4]

Third. St. Dismas was the only being who upon Calvary preached forth the divinity of Christ. The pleading of the Good Thief may be divided into two parts, In the first he proclaimed the innocence of our Lord: "This Man hath done no evil;" in the second, His divinity: "Remember me when Thou shalt come into *Thy kingdom.*" What kingdom is this, of which Dismas speaks? Not a kingdom of this world, evidently, for our Lord was on the point of death; but the kingdom of Heaven, that kingdom of which there shall be no end — which, through His death, Christ was about to reenter, and of which Dismas thus declared Him Lord and Master. And thus did this glorious evangelist make known the divinity of Jesus of Nazareth, for who is Lord of Heaven, but God alone?

Now, if great courage was necessary to assert the innocence of Christ, how much more to proclaim His Godhead? The first would indeed annoy and irritate the Jews, but this last would madden them with rage. At the same time, scorn and contempt would be largely mixed with their fury. "Fool," would they say "how can this malefactor remember thee? what kingdom will He have to dispose of, He that is guilty as thou art, and like thee, about to die? Thou proclaimest Him God, whereas, forsooth, He is less than man."

But Dismas heeded not their insulting cries. He believed, and thenceforth nothing could shake his hope nor cool his ardent love.

Ah! great indeed must have been that faith which gave such wonderful power of penetration to the hitherto benighted thief, that he was able clearly to discern the Godhead, hidden beneath the dishonored veil of the bruised and bleeding humanity of Christ. Surpassing great was that grace, which enabled him to put all his trust in a Man, whose pitiful condition announced rather the meanest of criminals, than the Desired of Nations. None, I think, will dare deny that this clear, firm, lively faith — a faith which inspired such a confession, at such a time and in such a place — was one of the greatest and most exceptionally precious graces which have ever been bestowed upon mortal man. For myself, I do not hesitate to consider it as one of the very greatest of the many privileges which God, in His mercy has deigned to heap upon our glorious saint. Verily and indeed, may we cry out with St. Augustine: "Christ hath not found so great faith in Israel, nay, nor in the whole world!"[5]

CHAPTER 24

The Glory of the Good Thief *(continued)*

W E have already described three of the exceptional privileges of the Good Thief. We now come to the fourth, which is this: that St. Dismas was the comforter of the Blessed Virgin in her sorrows. We have endeavored to realize, as far as the finite nature of our minds will allow, what is the gratitude of our divine Savior towards His daring advocate and defender. Hardly less lively is that of Mary for him who so powerfully soothed her sufferings, by taking upon himself the defense of her Son. Doubtless St. John and the holy women, who accompanied the Blessed Virgin, had done their best to comfort and support her amid her dire agony, but these dear friends said not a word which could lighten her burden of sorrow. During that whole day of heartrending suffering, she had listened unceasingly to the mockeries and blasphemies, and death cries of the wicked enemies of her Son; but not until Dismas spoke had she heard aught of comfort. To understand the efficacy of this balm upon her wounded heart, we ought to know the depth of those wounds, the measure of her love. Her Jesus, who had been calumniated, and buffeted, and spat upon, and as a malefactor and seducer condemned to die the cruelest and most shameful of deaths, was now at last recognized and proclaimed not only as the innocent Lamb, but very God; the Creator and Redeemer; the Desired of Nations, the looked-for Messias!

The words of the Good Thief showed her that her Son's death was already bearing fruit, that He had already drawn to Himself at least one soul, and that this one was not only faithful, like St. John, but bold and fearless in giving testimony to His Godhead. By thus proclaiming, in the sight of Heaven and earth, the innocence and the divinity of Christ, Dismas satisfied Mary's chief longing, the most earnest desire of her soul.

St. Bernardine of Siena is of the opinion that our saint was not content with thus indirectly ministering to her comfort. He says: "There is nothing to prevent our believing that having survived the death of Jesus, and seeing the bitterness of His mother's grief, he addressed to her words full of compassion and filial love, showing thereby that he held her to be truly his mother also; for, knowing himself to have been redeemed by Christ, he doubted not that he had become the adopted son of his Lord's Virgin Mother."[1]

Thus we may say that Dismas was in an especial manner the privileged companion and comforter of the Mother of God. The love of Mary for her Son was a twofold love. In her Son, she loved her God; and in her God, her Son. Of these two loves — the natural and the supernatural love, each carried to their very highest pitch of perfection — was borne on Calvary that sorrow spoken of by the prophet, a sorrow greater than all sorrow, like unto which there is none other. Now, the sorrow Dismas felt at the death of Christ had some faint resemblance to this in kind, if not in degree; for if he had no nearer relation to Him than that which all those redeemed bear to their Savior, and every creature to its Maker, yet he at least resembled Mary in this, that he wept in Christ crucified the Man-God, dying for the salvation of the world. And this clear knowledge, which at the time was possessed among men by him alone, was what earned for him the rare privilege of sharing in so great a measure the sorrows of our Blessed Lady.

True, that St. John and St. Mary Magdalen were there on Calvary together with the Mother of God, and taking part in her inexpressible grief. " But," says St. Bernardine, "though they wept bitterly over their dying Master, they did not weep over Him as their God, dying for the salvation of the human race. Whence their lament was far from having the requisite perfection. Therefore the tears of this thief were alone worthy to be accepted with those of Mary, because he alone, with Heaven-born faith, really and firmly believed Him to be God Whom, with unspeakable sorrow, he saw before his eyes as a dying man."[2]

And so glorious does this privilege appear to the angel of Siena, that he loves to come back to it, again and again. In another place, comparing Dismas with the Apostles, he says: "Everywhere they had heard (Christ) preaching; on all sides they had seen His miracles; and, but a little while before, they had received from His hands, His most holy Body as their food; and yet they denied Him, by taking to flight. And this man alone, with the silent Virgin, in his soul believed with unswerving faith that He was the Son of God."[3]

The blessed Simon of Cassia gives expression to the same thought: "Alone, the thief confessed in speech, Him Whom Mary silently worshipped; and in the midst of his terrible sufferings he became the companion of the Virgin's faith, as of her woe."[4] And Padre Orilia further adds: "In this supreme hour of the Passion of Christ, the faith of all, excepting only Mary, had faltered, if it had not even been destroyed."[5]

Moreover, the Gospel itself tells us that the Apostles were full of uncertainty and doubt, even after Easter day; disbelieving the resurrection of their Master, and consequently the truth of His promises, and His very Godhead. Thus we find them affrighted, instead of rejoiced, at the evidence given thereof by the holy women, and treating their words as idle tales. And when at length He deigned to appear to the eleven, He upbraided them with their unbelief and hardness of heart. Even after that, they more than once took Him for a spirit, and were afraid. To convince them, it was necessary for Him to condescend to eat with them, and to allow them to touch His sacred body, and to feel the place of the wounds.(Mk 16:11,13,14 ; Lk 24:11,25,37,41)

With such an indisputable record before us of the Apostles' want of faith, and of the misconceived notions of Magdalen and the other women, we may safely conclude, with the writers we have already cited, that the Mother of God and the converted thief alone preserved their faith intact throughout the fiery trial of Calvary; yet so, Mary was not alone in her grief. In however small a measure, that grief was shared by Dismas. Enlightened by faith, he believed without doubting that Christ was as truly God as Man. Wherefore, in weeping over His sufferings, he wept also for the sacrilegious guilt of the Deicidal Jews, and weeping, worshipped; and, by the greatness of his love, strove to wash away their ingratitude.

Now, where throughout the history of the Church shall we find any saint possessed of so great and wonderful a privilege? At the time of our Lord's death, there were in Jerusalem great numbers of elect souls, Christ's beloved disciples — His friends, those whom He had chosen to be the princes of His Church — and yet, not one of them was found whose faith was like to that of the thief. Not one was permitted to share, as he did the unspeakable sorrows of Mary and her unearthly love for the Man-God, her Son.

The fifth privilege of St. Dismas consists in this, that he was the type and figure of all the elect.[6] The doom of the thieves on Calvary has always been looked upon by the fathers of the Church as a foreshadowing of the great judgment to come. Then, as at the last day, him saved is on the right of Christ, ready to ascend with Him to Heaven: the impenitent sinner on the left, about to fall down into the gaping jaws of hell. In the midst, the Man-God, Judge of the quick and the dead, upon the gibbet — now become a throne of glory — rendering to every man according to his works. Now, as the bad thief was the type and figure of the lost, so was the Good Thief the type and figure of the elect.

Great and worthy of respect is the ambassador of some powerful monarch. But how much greater is he who represents not one earthly king, but thousands, or rather countless myriads of heavenly princes. Such greatness is that of Dismas, who, by a special prerogative, was chosen to represent on the cross all the saints, who shall ever reign with God in Heaven. In him, and in him alone, at that most solemn moment did the unsearchable, immeasurable mercy of God show itself forth; that mercy which calls all men, and rewards those who obey the call with the ineffable delights of the Beatific Vision. To him were first addressed those blessed, glorious words: "This day shalt thou be with Me in Paradise."

The Apostles were destined to hear them one day, but not yet. Thousands of saints and martyrs have heard them since, and gladly have they entered into the joy of their Lord. These words form the hope of many who are struggling in this land of exile amidst poverty and work and woe; they are a promise of life to generations yet unborn; and on the great final day shall be the password of those redeemed, of every tribe and nation. To no saint, save Dismas, has it been given to hear these consoling words till after death. The greatest have worked out their salvation in fear and trembling, while thinking to stand taking heed lest they should fall; but to Dismas the certainty of final perseverance was given at the same time as the pardon of his sins, and the promise added thereto, unconditionally. There could be no mistake; no room was left for presumption or for doubt. The words were uttered by God Himself, in the presence of a countless multitude, in the hearing of the whole Court of Heaven.

How exceptional was this glorious privilege may be gathered from the fact that our Lord never bestowed it even upon his most favored, not even upon the beloved disciple. Yet more, He actually refused it when asked by his kinswoman, the mother of the sons of Zebedee. When she begged of Him that her sons might sit in His Kingdom, the one on His right hand the other on His left, He rebuked her, saying: "You know not what you ask." And questioning them, He said: "Can you drink the chalice that I shall drink?" And they answered: "We can." Yet even so, He gave not the promise, but said: "My chalice indeed you shall drink, but to sit on my right or left hand is not mine to give to you, but to them for whom it is prepared by my Father." (Mt 20:20,23)

Thus we may safely say, with St. Chrysostom, that this great privilege was reserved for our saint, and for him alone. "Thou findest none," he rapturously exclaims, "worthy to enter the promised Paradise before the thief — not even Abraham, nor Isaac, nor Jacob, nor Moses, nor the Prophets, nor the Apostles, but, before all, Thou receivest the thief."[7]

And in another place the same great Doctor asks: "What is this mystery? How is it that a robber should be the first to receive the promise of Paradise? Whence is this that a murderer should before all others become a citizen of Heaven? Behold the reason thereof. The first man was a robber, guilty of having stolen the forbidden fruit — he was driven out of Paradise. The convert of Calvary was also a robber. But because he hath taken of the fruit of the tree of the Cross, he has been brought back before all others into Paradise. As sin came through means of the wood, even so cometh salvation.

"God so willed it to teach all men that if, like the thief, they will adore Christ crucified as their Lord and God, so, like him, they shall receive the same reward. He willed it thus, that, seeing Him from the Cross forgive the robber all his sins, men should believe that He, the Universal Redeemer, has blotted out the sentence of condemnation which had been pronounced upon the human race. He willed it for the sake of showing that if in the guilty person of Adam, mankind had, as a wild briar, been put out of Paradise, so, in the person of the penitent thief it had been replanted there as a rose tree."[8]

"And thus promising him Heaven for that same day, He made him at the same time the figure and the precursor of all those who, through the merits of the Redemption, shall enter into the royal abodes of the Blessed Jerusalem."

From these privileges of St. Dismas, we can form some faint idea of the glory which he enjoys in Heaven. "Grace," says St. Thomas, "is in us but the beginning of glory."[9] The greater, the more sublime, and the more wonderful the grace which is given to man on his journey through this land of exile, the greater and the more perfect will be the glory and happiness which he shall receive in his heavenly Home.[10] Starting from these premises, and having before our eyes the extraordinary and boundless nature of the graces poured upon the Good Thief, we may conclude that his glory is something so great as to pass our understanding. Fitly, may we apply to him the mysterious words of St. Paul: "Eye hath not seen, nor ear heard, nor hath it entered into the heart of man to conceive," the happiness, glory, power, and majesty which God hath given as an everlasting heritage to this well-beloved fellow sufferer and confessor of His Son.

It is not for us to seek to dive into the hidden counsels of the Providence of God. Still I may here observe that many of the holy doctors of the Church, knowing that the Divine Wisdom always provides means commensurate with the end It has in view, have not scrupled to affirm and to teach that the Good Thief now reigns upon one of the highest thrones of the Heavenly Jerusalem. "When," says St. Bernardine of Siena, "being crushed down by grief and suffering upon the wine press of the Cross, our good Jesus let flow without stint the precious wine of His love, which was to make glad the heart of man, He was not content with giving, as it were, a small drink of it to the Good Thief; but uniting his blessed soul to His own divine Heart, He filled it and, so to speak, drowned it in love — so that I doubt not but what this brave defender of our Lord now shines among the highest princes in the Court of the Heavenly King."[11]

Another great writer does not hesitate to speak of Dismas as the Archangel of Paradise, the first-born of Christ Crucified, the greatest of martyrs, the chief of apostles, the universal preacher. And he adds: "If Paul speaks like the cherubim, Dismas, we may say, loves like the seraphim."[12] And that pious and learned friend of St. Bernard, Arnold of Chartres, says that he is seated upon the very throne of Lucifer himself.[13]

And there seems no reason why this should not be the case. What other is more worthy of this throne? On the one hand, we know that the thrones of Lucifer and his rebel angels are to be given to God's elect among men, and that as in his army there were spirits of every rank, so the just made perfect will be made to sit down among the cherubim and seraphim as among every other choir of the celestial hierarchy. And, on the other hand, we know that the Good Thief was chosen to represent the whole human race; that he was the most fearless of all the disciples; that he was the faithful companion of our Lord's sufferings and of our Lady's sorrows; that he was the first to receive the promise of Paradise. We know, moreover, that his faith, his hope, and his charity, all and each, attained the highest possible degree of heroic perfection. Why, therefore, should it not be fitting that he who was the first to enter Heaven, should occupy there the first place among the saints, even the throne of the fallen Light-Bearer, the first tempter of mankind?

Be this as it may, for ourselves, we never can sufficiently understand and admire the power of repentance, nor can we ever sufficiently admire and worship the infinite goodness of our God. Such is His mercy, that in a moment, in the twinkling of an eye, He cleanses a soul deep-dyed in guilt and stained with every sin, and makes it worthy to take rank among the highest and purest of the heavenly spirits. One thing alone He asks — repentance. Ah! who shall have the folly to refuse it? Let us all learn of Dismas, that, like him, we too may receive an eternal reward. "He was a straw fit for Tartarus, he is become a cedar of Paradise — a brand of Hell, now a shining light in the firmament of Heaven."[14] We, too, may have been separated from the good wheat, and may have been already cast out; but the final hour of condemnation is not yet, and let us not forget that God is waiting, ready to snatch us as a brand from the burning.

CHAPTER 25

What Became of the Relics of the Good Thief

THE bodies of our Lord and of the two thieves were taken down from the cross immediately after their death and hurriedly buried, on account of the Sabbath, which began about sunset. Such was the law of the Jews. One of the Rabbinical writers explains it in the following terms: "The law does not suffer malefactors to pay with money that which they ought to pay with their lives, or at least with exile. On the contrary, the law rigorously exacts blood for blood, and requires the death of the murderer in expiation of the death of his victim. If it were otherwise, murder would become rife and every other crime would be freely committed.[1] Against such evil-doers, the legislator would, if it had been possible, have decreed a thousand deaths; as it was, however, he commanded that they should be crucified, this being the worst known form of death.

"Nevertheless, Moses, the meekest and gentlest of men, showed mercy even to these men of blood. 'Let not the sun set,' he says, 'upon those who are hanged upon a gibbet, but let them be taken down and buried before the day end.' In their punishment, two things were necessary. First, it was necessary to lift up those who by their crimes had stained every part of creation — that Heaven and earth, the sun and the air, should all alike be witness of their chastisement. And secondly, it was necessary promptly to hide them away in the earth, that they should no longer soil anything visible."

In accordance, therefore, with the law, and because of the great Sabbath day which was at hand, the body of the Good Thief was taken down from the cross as soon as the *crurifragium* had deprived it of the last vestiges of life, and hurriedly buried upon the hill of Calvary. Together with, or near to, his body were likewise buried the instruments of his death.

"It appears from the Talmud," says Baronius, "and from the writings of the Rabbim Jacob Surim, and Moses Ægyptius, that it was forbidden to bury the corpses of criminals in the common burial ground; they had to be put in some private place apart. And in the same manner the instruments of death were also to be separately buried — namely, the crosses, nails, swords, or stones, according to the form of punishment. For this reason, it was forbidden to crucify any one to a tree, and it was ordered that a cross should be cut out of the wood, that it might be afterwards buried with the other implements of death."[2]

After the execution of Calvary, the Jews threw the three crosses into one and the same pit, where they remained for three hundred years, until discovered by the saintly mother of the first Christian emperor.

As is well known, this discovery was effected under the greatest difficulties. Since the taking of Jerusalem by Titus, the pagan Romans had done their best to obliterate every trace of our Lord's crucifixion, and for this purpose huge loads of earth had been brought and deposited on the top of Calvary, making a sort of artificial summit of great depth. This they surrounded with a wall, which they covered with pagan emblems, and within they paved the whole space and raised in the midst of it a temple to Venus, and close by, a statue of Jupiter.

Hence, any Christians going to pray on Mount Calvary, were looked upon as having worshipped idols. So that fear of being taken for idolaters kept them back, and the sacred place was entirely deserted, and given up to the abominations of paganism. The enemies of God, seeing the success of their scheme, rejoiced in the vain hope that, the holy place being abandoned, the memory of those things which were done there would also die out. But in the blind folly of their so-called wisdom, the Romans were only seconding, and, indeed, working out, the hidden designs of Providence. By covering over and hiding the site of the crucifixion, they preserved the Cross of our Lord until such time as the Church should be at peace; for, had it been brought forth during the ages of persecution, it would doubtless have been profaned and destroyed.

When St. Helena arrived on pilgrimage at the Holy City, she was nowise held back by the many obstacles which offered themselves to the fulfillment of her pious designs. A great number of workmen and soldiers were at once set to work to pull down the temple and statue, and to clear away the soil piled up on the top of the mount. The work was done with such great zeal and activity that, in a short time, the natural summit of the hill was discovered and set free. Then remained the more difficult question as to the precise spot where the crosses had been buried. To obtain an answer to this, the Empress diligently consulted the traditions current among both Jews and Christians. For some time no clear information could be obtained; but at last she was informed that the Jews knew the place, but refused to point it out.

We cannot here do better than give the letter of the Emperor Leo to Umarus, King of the Saracens, which contains a most interesting account of what took place. This letter is not generally much known; though it deserves to be so, as adding several precious details to what we know, through St. Paulinus and St. Ambrose, and other ecclesiastical writers, on the subject of the finding of the holy Cross.

Here is the text of the letter: "I will now make answer to the question you have addressed to me concerning Jesus Christ. He was crucified between two thieves — the one on His right hand, the other on His left — and died the same day. And at once the earth quaked, and the sun refused its light. The princes of the

Jews, who were present, were seized with a great fear, and would willingly have hidden every trace of what had just taken place. For this reason, they hid away the crosses on which the bodies had been hung, and buried them in the ground, and none knew the place where they had put them, except only one of their number. During life, he was never to mention the secret to any human being, nor until the approach of death, when he was allowed to tell one of his near relations, saying to him that if ever the Cross should be demanded of them, there he would find it.

"When Jesus Christ had resolved publicly to confound the Jews, He showed the Cross to Constantine, Emperor of the Romans, who at that time was not a Christian. The apparition was in this wise. As he was going to battle, he suddenly saw in the heavens two columns, suspended in the air in the form of a cross, and on these columns an inscription of dazzling brightness. This inscription contained the following words, written in Greek: 'Because thou hast asked of God to show thee the true faith — make to thyself an imperial standard on the model of this Cross, and cause it to be borne before thee at the head of thine army.' The Emperor obeyed, attacked his enemy, and gained over him a complete victory by the power of the holy Cross.

"On his return, he sent Helena, his mother, with a band of soldiers, to Jerusalem, and demanded of the Jews what had become of the Cross of the Lord. As they refused to answer, she had many of them put to the torture. At last they told her which among them, it was, who was possessed of the secret. The Empress at once sent for him to come before her. On his refusing to give the required information, he was let down into a pit, and then left without food or drink. At the end of several days, when he was nearly dying, he at last consented to show the place where the crosses lay buried.

" Immediately they began to dig down, and presently there came out of the hole a sweet-smelling odor, and in a short time the three crosses were found, which had been hidden there for three hundred years. The Empress, not knowing which was the cross of the Lord, ordered that all three should be made to touch the body of a dead man. The touch of the first and of the second had no effect, but, as soon as the third had been laid upon him, the dead man arose, full of life. The Empress built a church over the sepulcher of Jesus Christ, and deposited there a portion of the true cross; the rest she brought to her son."

History has preserved to us the name of the Jew, who betrayed the secret of his co-religionists — he was called Judas. Seeing the miracles that were done, he became a convert to Christianity and changed his name to that of Cyriac, became a Bishop, and died as a martyr, under Julian the Apostate. His feast is marked for the 1st of May, in Bede's Martyrology. We find the history of his conversion in Gregory of Tours, and in several other writers quoted by Gretzer.

After mentioning this testimony, the learned monk adds: "This history must not be looked upon as spurious, not only because of the authority of Gregory of Tours, but much more because of the liturgical office for the Finding of the Holy Cross,[3] in which we find exactly the same account of this Judas — an office which is yearly recited by all ecclesiastics."[4]

As we learn from the fathers and from the above cited letter of the Emperor Leo, the cure of a dying, and the raising up of a dead man, proved with certainty and beyond all doubt which of the three crosses was that of the Savior. They do not, it is true, speak of any miracle in connection with the cross of the Good Thief. If any such had occurred at that time, it would only have served to prevent the identification of the true Cross. Therefore it is very easy to account for their silence. But their silence is no proof that miracles were not so wrought at another time; at the most, it is but a negative proof, and cannot be made use of to overthrow the positive testimony of those who, without some supernatural sign, could have had no means of distinguishing the cross of the Good Thief, from that of the bad thief. Now, as relics of the cross of St. Dismas are religiously preserved and venerated, both in East and West, we cannot suppose them to be other than well-authenticated, without insult to the common sense and piety of thousands of eminent Christians of both ancient and modern times.

Now we know, upon the authority of history, that St. Helena, while at Jerusalem, made a collection of whatever objects had been sanctified by the Savior's touch, or had been associated with any of His miracles, or with events recorded in the Old Testament. Many of these latter objects were still in existence in the fourth century, having been wonderfully preserved by the Providence of God, as corroborative proofs of the truth of the Mosaic recital. Most of these, such as the statue of salt which had once been Lot's wife, and the huge bones of the giants whose sins had called down upon them the Deluge — mention of which bones we have already made in another place, in the words of Josephus — most of these, I say, were left in the Holy Land, and, long after, carefully preserved there by both Jews and Christians.

But, on the other hand, all the relics which had any connection with the life or death of our Lord were taken, either whole or in part, to Constantinople, and there given by St. Helena to her son. Not only did the Empress take the greater portion of the true Cross, together with the nails, and title, and other instruments of the Sacred Passion, but also, likewise, the crosses of the two thieves. If both were not meant for the veneration of the faithful, both at least were interesting as having been connected with the greatest event of the world's history. If the one was a monument of the mercy of God, the other was no less a monument of His justice. If the one was like to inspire repentance, hope, and love; the other was fitted to excite fear of the divine judgments.

Among other things brought to Constantinople by St. Helena was the alabaster box which contained the ointment made use of by Magdalen; the twelve baskets, and those other seven, in which the fragments were placed of the miraculously multiplied loaves and fishes; and even a few pieces of those said loaves. There was also the axe used by Noah in the building of the ark. All these things were received by Constantine, with great joy and veneration. To house them with fitting splendor, he built a very beautiful shrine, consisting of four solid archways delicately worked, the pillars of which formed, as it were, four apses, and in the midst was a superb column of porphyry, hollowed out so as to hold the rich casket containing these precious relics. The relics were then sealed up by Constantine himself, with the great seal of the Empire. The shrine is described by the Greek historian, Nicephorus, who tells us that in his day it was still in a perfect state of preservation.[5] It is spoken of also by many other eminent Greek writers.[6]

It would seem, from an undoubtedly ancient and well authenticated tradition, that only a small portion of the Cross of St. Dismas ever reached Constantinople, the greater part of it having been given by St. Helena to the inhabitants of Cyprus, when she touched at that island, on her way back from the Holy Land. For centuries it was kept in a monastery, situated among the mountains, near Nicosia, the ancient capital, now called Lefkosia.

It was placed behind the high altar of the monastery church, where, tradition says, it remained suspended in mid-air. This was variously attributed, says Lucas Tudensis, to miraculous, or ingeniously artificial, causes. The wise and learned bishop refrains from giving his own opinion, contenting himself with mentioning the phenomenon. He adds that, having encased the Good Thief's cross with silver, the Empress enshrined in it a portion of the Cross of our Lord. Dismas' cross, so enriched, was held in the highest veneration, and the convent where it was placed became the chief and favorite resort of all Cypriot pilgrims. On certain days, the church was thronged with great crowds that came thither from every part of the island. Miracles were said to be often wrought there, and, certain it is, that many and great graces were obtained through the intercession of St. Dismas, as well as through the wonder-working power of the Cross of Christ.

Of that portion of the cross of the Good Thief which was taken to Constantinople, many small fragments were cut off and given away as precious treasures to various churches of both East and West. One of these relics is now kept in the basilica of Santa

Cruce in Jerusaleme, at Rome. It may be seen on the altar of the Chapel of the Relics, where it is enshrined in a reliquary of crystal. At Bologna, also, is still to be found a large piece of this same cross. It is in the beautiful church of SS. Vitalis and Agricola. The inhabitants of this learned city have always been remarkable for their devotion to our saint. But, that they were not singular in their devotion, will be seen in the following chapter.

NOTE — It may not be out of place to give here some explanation of the practice of venerating relics, as authorized and approved of by the Church. I will do so in the words of the learned Barnabite, Father Tondini de Quarenghi. "In regard to the danger of superstition, I would observe that no Catholic who knows his Catechism would ever think that there was any *inherent* virtue whatsoever in dead portions of the body of a saint, or in other relics. The miracles which, in common parlance, are said to have been worked by such or such relics, have not in truth been worked by the relics but by God. This no Catholic would doubt. To tonel (or kiss) relics, or to say *before them* prayers which are addressed (not to them but) to the *saints living in Heaven*, these are but part of the various modes we have of expressing our belief in God, and in the doctrine of the intercession of saints. This faith it is which God rewards even by the working of miracles. Hence the authenticity of the relic is after all but a secondary matter, the prayers of the faithful being addressed not to the relic itself but to the *living being* to whom it may have belonged. I need hardly add that the respect shown to a relic is *necessarily* dependent upon the question of its authenticity, and is only paid subject to this condition, which must *always* be present at least implicitly in the mind of every Catholic."

See *Règlement* ecclésiastique de Pierre le Grand: avec Introduction, etc., par le P. C. Tondini, Barnabite, etc., etc. Paris, Libr. de la Société Bibl., 35, Rue de Grenelle, pp. 41, 42. — TR.

CHAPTER 26

On Devotion to the Good Thief

DEATH cannot break the bond of love which unites the saints of Time with those of Eternity — the Christians still struggling on earth with the just made perfect, who are already reaping their reward in the Heavenly Kingdom. For the saints of God, death is, as it were, a new birth, the awakening to eternal life. Hence the true Jerusalem is called the Land of the Living — *Terra Viventium.* And, in the language of the church, the birthday of a saint is that which, in ordinary parlance, is styled the day of his death — the day, that is, on which he quitted this outward, perishable shell, and, setting aside corruption, put on immortality.

Speaking of Abraham, and Isaac, and Jacob, our Lord said of old: "God is not the God of the dead, but of the living." What He said of them, is true of all the saints. And because they live, they love also, and hear, and see, and do. They are our brethren, members of the same family, of the same body, which is Christ's — and can we for a moment suppose that they are forgetful of us, whom they have left behind? If the angels, who are of another order of creation, rejoice over the conversion of sinners, how much more those who are bone of our bone, and flesh of our flesh? As says the great St. Cyprian: "Having secured their own undying happiness, they are still solicitous for our salvation."

From the very earliest times all true Christians have cherished this beautiful and most consoling belief. Far from its being in anyway displeasing to God, by detracting even in the smallest degree from the adorable, infinite, merits of our one, only, Savior; experience has shown that God sanctions, and I may say encourages it, by the graces, countless as the stars of Heaven, which He is ever giving us in answer to the prayers of the saints, whose intercession we have invoked. And, if God thus deigns to allow His saints to be the means of conveying to us many of His gifts, is it not right and just that we should pay to them as large a measure of thanks and devotion as may be consistent with looking upon them always as the distributors, not the authors, of the blessings we receive through them? Nature and grace alike demand of us this tribute of gratitude and love. Ay, and willingly we pay it, for are not these saints our fathers, and our brethren? Devotion to them is approved by our intellect, but much more is it enshrined in our hearts. Protestantism — in striving to deprive us of it — would, in truth, albeit unconsciously, break up the Communion of Saints, and indeed thereby shows itself to be as opposed to good feeling as it is to sound reason.

As a true and tender Father, God loves all the saints, His children, with an unspeakable, infinite love; but there are some who, by their greater merits, are nearer and dearer to Him than the rest. Now those whom He specially delights to honor, ought to receive from us also, a large measure of devotion. And among this number we need not, I think, hesitate to count the blessed Dismas. Of him it may be truly said, that, in a short space, he accomplished a long time; for, in the few hours of his spiritual life, he reached a higher degree of perfection than other saints have attained after long years of patient toil.

We have already given many and copious extracts from the fathers and other ecclesiastical writers in praise of the Good Thief. We cannot resist giving one more such passage. It is from the great St. Athanasius, and is taken from one of his admirable sermons. In this string of glowing invocations, the holy doctor sufficiently shows us his admiration and love for our saint. Let us repeat them with the same fervor.

"O blessed Thief! thou wert more swift to gain Heaven, than Adam was to lose it. The ill-advised father of the human race stretched forth his hand to take the fruit of the forbidden tree, and, in tasting thereof, sucked in the poison of death, which he has passed down to all his children. But thou, better advised, betaking thee to the sacred tree of the Cross, didst obtain Heaven, which thou hadst lost by thy sins, and, so, didst gain life everlasting.

"O blessed Thief! by finding out a secret, hitherto unknown, Thou hast carried off the greatest and best of treasures!

"O blessed Thief! truly didst thou copy the treachery of Judas, but him whom thou didst betray was the devil — thy crafty and implacable foe.

"O blessed Thief! who of thine heroic virtues didst make of thy cross a ladder wherewith to scale the heavens — a most speaking pulpit, whence thou didst preach forth with unearthly power the innocence and Godhead of thy beloved Savior.

"O blessed Thief! who didst triumphantly show to all the sinners of the world the power of faith and the efficacy of a well-made confession, and sincere repentance."[1]

The five glorious privileges of the Good Thief, which we have already explained, more than justify the greatness of these praises. May they wake up in us a true and ardent devotion! The power of the saints is in proportion to the rank they hold in Heaven. The higher a saint is lifted up in glory, the larger is the share vouchsafed him of the power, as of the happiness, of God. Now he that shall measure the glory of the blessed Dismas, he, and he alone, can tell us what should be the measure of the trust we may place in his intercession. But no man can rule, or compass, things unseen. Nevertheless, the Church is able to teach her children, approximately at least, what honor is due to each one of the saints, whose mother she likewise is.

Now, both in East and West, she has seen fit to approve and encourage great devotion towards the Good Thief. It is, therefore, hard for us to understand how it has come to pass that, in so many places, at the present day, this devotion has fallen into so great disuse. By the blessing of God, we would now humbly strive to revive, what should never have been forgotten.

The Feast of the Good Thief is variously kept, in the different Churches. The Churches of Syria and of Mesopotamia celebrate it on the ninth day after the Friday of the Dolors — that is, Saturday in Easter week; the Greeks on the 23rd of March; and, we Latins, on the 25th of the same month. In old days, the feast was kept with great pomp in most of the dioceses of the West. All the beautiful traditions which have come down to us concerning this great saint were to be found in the Lessons of the Day. In the ancient Breviary of Quimper, they are given at great length. In that, the feast is marked for the 26th of March. In the Martyrology of Usuardus, these lessons are appointed to be read on the 5th of May. The feast was kept in many places on that day. According to Molanus and Canisius, it was observed with special devotion at the Cathedral Church of Bruges, and, indeed, in most of the Churches.[2]

Such was the devotion paid the Good Thief, down to the sixteenth century. At the present day, unhappily, it is much less widespread than it was then; yet has it not died out altogether. Ah! let us do what in us lies to fan the yet flickering flame, that it may burn up once more into a fire of love, whereby men's hearts may be warmed towards God,

After the revision of the Roman Breviary, ordered by the Council of Trent, the *Order of our Lady of Mercy,* for the Redemption of Captives, was the first to ask for a new office in honor of the Good Thief. It was granted them by Sixtus V.

In the beginning of the eighteenth century, the Congregation of Devout Workmen (*Pii operai)* also obtained leave to keep the Feast of the Good Thief, with its proper office; and, in consequence of the many graces received through his intercession, they also chose him as their special advocate and patron. They had indeed good reason for gratitude towards him, and they were not slow to show it. At Naples, in the Church of St. George, they have a splendid chapel dedicated to our saint. The walls of this chapel are all covered with ex-votos, each of which bears witness to some great grace either of conversion or cure. The fathers of the Congregation are continually receiving letters expressive of gratitude for favors so obtained, and they find it hard to satisfy the unceasing demands of those who wish for pictures and other representations of the Good Thief.

The *Oblates of Mary,* those zealous missionaries who so fervently preach the Gospel in every part of the New as of the Old World, likewise recite this office. They do so from the same motives, and with the same happy results. We may say as much of the *Servites of Mary,* who fitly honor him, who shared the sorrows of the Mother of God, and was her best earthly comforter. We must not forget to mention the sons of the great St. Gaetano, of Thiena, who did so much for the revival of Catholicism in the sixteenth century. The Clerks Regular keep the Feast of the Good Thief on the 26th day of March. With them it is a double.

The devotion to St. Dismas has not, however, been entirely relegated to the interior of religious houses. It is still very popular in the South of Italy. In many families, it is customary to place his picture or statue above the entrance-door of their houses, and many wonderful histories are told of the efficacy of his protection. He is always invoked as against thieves and robbers.

Among all the cities of the South, Gallipoli, in the Gulf of Tarentum, is specially remarkable for the fervor of its devotion. The sailors of the coast never think of starting on a voyage or fishing expedition without first visiting the shrine of the Good Thief and invoking his blessing upon their enterprise; and, on their return, their first care is to make there a pilgrimage of thanksgiving. This devotion is by no means a new thing. It dates back many hundreds of years — to the time when the inhabitants of those parts were in constant danger from the lawless incursions of the pirates of Barbary. Then it was that the Converted Thief was chosen patron of the city. It was fitting that he, the one-time brigand-chief, should be called upon to defend the faithful from the attacks of those who were his followers in the paths of crime.

In all the country round about Gallipoli, are to be found numerous oratories and wayside chapels dedicated to St. Dismas. How is it that, in other Catholic lands, so little devotion should be paid to one who is so great in glory — to one whom our

Savior honored by taking him into Paradise, the very first day the gates thereof were reopened to men? Some, perhaps, might jeeringly reply that his protection is not everywhere so much needed. Yet I know of no country so happy as to be entirely free from every kind of theft. But even were it so — I do not speak of housebreaking and highway robbery only, such things are, God knows, common enough; but there is a more subtle, and, for that very reason, far more dangerous form of offence against the seventh commandment: I speak of those too common thefts of innocence, and of that most precious treasure of all, men's faith. Now how many are there whose chief object in life seems to be to despoil others of those blessings which they themselves are too blind to value! Much cause have we, therefore, to call for aid to the Good Thief. Moreover we have, alas! too faithfully copied him in his sins. We are, what he has been. Let us, then, copy his repentance, that through his prayers we may become, one day, what he now is! And we must not think of ourselves alone; we must think of our fellow sinners, whom we must strive to rescue as brands from the burning. Now what more consoling, what more hope-inspiring thought can we bring before a dying sinner than the thought of the blood-stained thief, repenting and pardoned upon the cross. No man had ever sinned more deeply, no man had ever lived a life more utterly forgetful of God; yet none has ever been more graciously received by Christ, or more perfectly forgiven. This thought should assuredly be to all sinners a source of unfailing hope, and a sure guarantee against that worst and most unpardonable of sins, despair. Ah! strange, indeed, does it seem that so little should be said by Catholic preachers on this subject; a subject wherein we find the most touching and convincing proof of the infinite greatness of the mercy of God.

That such neglect is contrary to the spirit of the Church may be proved by the constant use she makes of the Good Thief's example, as recorded for our teaching and comfort in the beautiful hymn for the dead. By this we are reminded, on the saddest and most solemn occasions, that we need not, must not, despair of the salvation of even the worst of sinners. Our Mother, the Church, bids us be of good heart and set all our trust in Him, who quencheth not the smoking flax nor breaks the bruised reed. She reminds us of His past mercies, that we may learn to look for the mercy to come. She urges us humbly to set before Him, His loving-kindness towards Magdalen and Dismas as the strongest plea for our own forgiveness. *"Qui Mariam absolvisti, et latronem exaudisti, mihi quoque spem dedisti."*[3] Thou who didst pardon Mary, and didst hearken to the Thief — to me, likewise, givest hope.

Now, although the conversion of the Good Thief is to us a chief source of hope, it is no ground for presumption; exceeding blind and foolish would that man be, who should be encouraged thereby to count upon a death-bed repentance. What right would he have to expect that time should then be given him? God is not patient forever, "He that holds out pardon," says St. Augustine, "does not promise the morrow."

Moreover, the conversion of Dismas was a great and astounding miracle. Miracles are by no means common; they are something rare and exceptional. They do not form part of the ordinary ways of divine Providence. To no man does God promise them; and much less to such as should tempt Him, by making such ill-grounded confidence an excuse for sin. Hence that other saying of St. Augustine: "There is one (robber, who repents), that thou shouldst not despair; he is but one, lest thou shouldst presume."

It is not, therefore, for the sake of lulling sinners into a dream of false security that we insist so strongly upon the conversion of the Good Thief — God forbid! Our aim is rather to show, by the blessing of God, that His mercy endureth for ever; that it is boundless, inexhaustible; that no life has been so deeply stained by crime as to have become incapable of a good end; that no sinner, when he shall be on the point of death, need give himself up to despair — in a word, that the example of the thief, converted upon the cross at the last hour of his life, has been thrown out, as it were, as an anchor of salvation to dying sinners, who were ready to fall into the bottomless pit of final impenitence.

Let us, once again, give ear to the voice of the fathers of the Church. The great Bishop Eusebius says: "In the person of our Lord Jesus Christ, God reconciled the world unto Himself — that is, His Godhead worked (out our Salvation) through means of His mortal body. His manhood was seen in the weakness of its own nature. His Godhead showed itself forth in the power of Its might. As man, He dies and goes down into hell. As God, He rises again triumphant. For the sake of saving the guilty, He allows Himself to be placed in the midst of the wicked: one is on His right hand, the other on His left. Through the agony of the cross, the Just One merits glory for one of the thieves. Now, if we look well into it, we shall find that so great a grace has not been conferred on this thief for himself alone. By releasing so notorious a criminal, by remitting so huge a debt, the Savior-God has given surety for the safety of the human race.

"He wishes that the forgiveness of one reprobate, should serve for the comfort and the hope of all the people, and that thus this personal gift, should become a public benefit. Wherefore, we must believe, without doubting, that (the pardon) received by the thief in reward for his faith, is a source of hope and advantage to us also. The infinite goodness of our God gives freely those things which He foreknows shall be of general usefulness. Hence, if filled with trust in such great mercy, any among us should condemn his past crimes by a new and better life, and should love Christ with his whole heart, he shall have within himself a beginning of the Paradise of the thief; and he shall know that it shall be opened unto him."[4]

The following beautiful passage is from St. Chrysostom's famous letter to Theodore of Mopsuesta. "Such is the mercy of God toward men that He never rejects a sincere repentance. But if any should have fallen into the lowest depth of wickedness, and should desire to return thence to the path of virtue, He receiveth such a one and embraceth him, and leaveth nothing undone which may restore him to his first state. (And He showeth) yet even greater mercy, for if (the sinner) be not able to work out a full and perfect penance, He disdaineth not a short one — and, for this little, He giveth a reward exceeding great. . . . *Today,* saith (the Royal Prophet), *if ye shall hear his voice, harden not your hearts, as in the day of provocation.* Now "today" may be understood of our whole life — yea, even to the extremest limit of old age. For penitence is not measured by length of time, but by the dispositions of the heart. The Ninevites had not striven for many days that their sins should be forgiven them; but, in the short space of one day, all their iniquity was blotted out. And the thief did not a long time implore for Paradise; but that instant wherein he pronounced one word was enough for the sins of his whole lifetime to be washed away; so that he received the reward of trial before even the Apostles themselves."[5]

It is also for the sake of showing forth the riches of His boundless mercy, and to give heart to our weakness, and to strengthen our trust in Him, that God has sometimes allowed, and still does allow, the great and terrible falls of even great saints. We will content ourselves merely with citing the example of the prophet-king, the man after God's own heart. And we will do so in the eloquent words of St. Augustine, himself once a notorious sinner and afterwards one of the very greatest of the saints and doctors of the Church of Christ.

After speaking of the two heinous crimes committed by David, St. Augustine goes on to say: "Which things let men take heed to avoid. But if they should themselves have fallen, let us hear what it is they should copy. Many are fain to fall with David — yet will they not rise up with David. It is not the example of his fall which is set before thee, but of his rising up, if that thou (thyself) hast fallen. Take heed lest thou fall. Let not the fall of the strong be the delight of the weak, but their fear rather. For this is it set before us; for this is it written. For this is it so often read of and chanted in the Church; that those who have not fallen should beware, and that such as have fallen should rise up again. The sin of such a man is not passed over in silence, but is preached forth in the Churches. And wicked hearers listen, and seek to find a plea for sin; they look for an excuse for what

The Life of the Good Thief

they themselves are about to do, and not for a warning against what they have not yet done. And they say to themselves: If David (so transgressed) wherefore not I? Wherefore the soul which shall do these things because David did them shall be yet more guilty, for this is worse than what David did. I will explain myself, if possible, more clearly. David did not set up for himself, as thou dost, a model (of sin). He fell through lust; but not under the sanction (as it were) of holiness. But thou settest before thee a saint that thou mayest sin; thou copiest not his sanctity, but his ruin; thou dost love in David, what David hates in himself. Thou dost prepare thyself to sin; thou dost make thyself ready for sinning. Thou dost read the Book of God that thou mayest sin. Thou dost listen to the Word of God that so thou learn to offend God more. This David did not do. He was rebuked by the Prophet; he did not fall because of the Prophet.

"If any who should hear these things be already fallen, and have his conscience stained with evil, . . . let him indeed consider the greatness of his wound, but let him not doubt the healing power of the Physician. Sin, with despair, is certain death. Therefore let no man say: 'If I have already done evil, I am even now condemned — God forgiveth not such wickedness, why should I not heap up sin upon sin? . . . All hope of pardon is lost. I will at least enjoy what I see, if I cannot look to have that which I believe.' But this Psalm,[6] at the same time as it makes those wary who have not yet fallen, prevents those that have fallen from giving themselves up to despair. O thou who hast sinned, and dost hesitate to do penance for thy sin, despairing of thy salvation, listen to David's lament. To thee Nathan the prophet is not sent, but even David himself. Hear his cries, and do thou likewise cry out; mark his groans, and do thou sigh with him; see, he weeps, mingle thy tears with his; witness his conversion, and take part in his happiness. If he has not been able to shut thee off from sin, let him at least open to thee the hope of pardon."[7]

What St. Augustine here says of David applies with even greater force to the Good Thief. In looking at the one case the sinner might still doubt whether the forgiveness obtained by the

Psalmist might not in some sense be due to the holiness of his previous life, which might form some sort of claim, not upon the justice, but upon the mercy of God. Whereas, in the case of the Good Thief, his past was but one unbroken crime, without a single redeeming point — unless perchance that kind act of his towards the Holy Family in the desert. And who is there, however deep sunk in wickedness, who has not done at least one good deed during the course of his life? We may therefore, I think, safely point out Dismas as having been as thoroughly steeped in iniquity as it is possible for man to be; and then, comparing what he has been with what he now is, hold up his present glory and happiness as a motive for encouragement and hope to even the most guilty. In the words of St. Ambrose: "There is none whom it shall be possible to keep out (of Heaven) when the thief is received (there)." "Let no man therefore," says St. Chrysostom, "despair of salvation. For wickedness is not an evil inborn in nature; we are gifted with liberty and free will. Art thou a publican? Thou mayst become an evangelist. A blasphemer? Thou canst be an apostle. A thief? Thou canst possess thee of Paradise. A magician? Thou mayst worship the Lord. There is no crime (or vice) which may not be done away by penance. For which reason, Christ removed a very mountain of iniquity, that so henceforth there should be no room left open for doubt."[8]

Now, before bringing this book to a close, it may be as well to give one out of many instances, in which the power of Dismas, the companion of our Lord upon the Cross — or *fellow soldier of the Kingdom,* as St. Athanasius styles him — is miraculously shown forth.

Towards the end of the fourth century, the great St. Porphyrus, afterwards Bishop of Gaza, was living as a hermit on the banks of the Jordan. Being attacked by a fatal disease of the liver, he was rapidly wasting away. Feeling that his end was at hand, he had himself carried up to Jerusalem, that he might die in that sacred place where the Savior gave His life for the world. Notwithstanding his extreme weakness, he visited each day some one of the holy places. Being about to die, he remembered that when he gave up the world he had left a huge fortune at his home, which was at Thessalonica — not having given it away to the poor on account of the youth of his brethren. He accordingly sent thither his dear friend Mark, the Deacon, that he might set his affairs in order. And he, coming to Ascalon, took ship, and presently arrived at Thessalonica after a thirteen days' voyage; and, showing the written command given him by Porphyrus, he divided the share of goods which came to his lot equally with that of his brethren, and, selling the saint's portion of the lands, he brought away the sum so realized — partly in money and partly in precious stuffs — and returned to Jerusalem after an absence of three months. We will give the account of what then passed between him and St. Porphyrus in his own words:

"And when this blessed man saw me, he embraced me with joy and tears (for tears do also sometimes express joy), but I truly, knew him not; for his person looked well-favored and his face ruddy, and I kept gazing upon him, not being able to turn away mine eyes.

"But he, seeing this, smiled, and gently said to me 'Marvel not, brother Mark, to see me thus in health and strong, but learn the cause of my soundness, and do thou admire the wonderful bounty of Christ, with Whom it is easy to cure evils which to man appear utterly hopeless.'

"I therefore besought him that he should tell me the cause of his renewed health, and how it had chanced that this dire sickness had been driven out of him. And he, making answer, said unto me: 'Forty days from this time — it being the vigil of the Lord's holy day — great pain came upon me, and I, not being able to bear it, went and lay me down near to the place of Calvary, and being, through excess of suffering, ravished, as it were, out of myself, me-thought I saw the Savior, fixed to the cross with nails, and with Him one of the thieves, likewise hanging from a cross. And I began to cry out, and to say, in the words of the thief: "Lord, remember me, when Thou shall come into Thy Kingdom." And the Savior, answering, said to the hanging thief: "Get thee down from the cross and save him who lieth there upon the ground, even as thou thyself wast saved." And the thief, coming down from the cross, clasped me in his arms and kissed me, and, taking me by the right hand, made me rise up, saying: "Come to the Savior." And, forthwith, I arose and ran to Him, and I saw Him also come down from the cross, and He said to me: "Take this wood, and be thou healed." And when I had taken up this precious wood, and was carrying it, at once, I came back to myself out of mine ecstasy, and from that hour the pain left me, neither has any sign of the disease returned.'

"But I, having heard these things, was filled with exceeding great wonder, and I gave glory to God; and from that time forth I cleaved more to that man and served him the more diligently."[9]

And we, also, let us give glory to God, and let us cleave to and love that glorious saint, whom God deigned to use as his instrument for the cure of the blessed Porphyrus. Our bodies may, perchance, be sound; but our souls, do they not require the Physician's care? Are they not laboring under at least one disease — perhaps under a complication of many? Who knows but what they may be sick, yea, sick even unto death? And if we have repented of our sins, and they have already been forgiven us, and we have begun a new life, and are really striving to serve God with our whole heart; are there not many others, whom we love, whose sins we mourn over, and who have not yet turned to God? Every day we send up our prayers to Heaven for their conversion — during long years, maybe, in vain. True, our prayers have not been lost if they have been offered up in an earnest and humble spirit. But how often, alas! has the canker of mixed or evil motives, or want of faith and trust, well-nigh destroyed their worth! If, therefore, we be conscious of any such imperfection in our prayers — and who shall dare say otherwise? — shall we not do well to implore the help of others better than ourselves — of some who, without doubt, are nearer to God than we are? When God had chidden the friends of Job, because they had not spoken before Him the things that were right, and they began to repent, He commanded them to offer up for themselves a holocaust. But this was not enough.

He commanded them also to ask the prayers of his servant Job. And they "did as the Lord had spoken to them, and the Lord *accepted the face of Job.* The Lord also was turned at the *penance of Job, when he prayed for his friends."* (Job 43: 8-10) When two or three are gathered together in the name of Christ, their prayer has greater power than if they had offered it up separately. (Mt 18:20) But if God attaches so much weight to the prayers of good men, who are still in a state of probation — of how much more avail must be the prayers of the just made perfect, who have run their course, whose fight is over and won, and who have already put on the unfading crown of glory.

We may address ourselves at choice to any of the heavenly company — all are members with us of One body, Christ; all form part of the Communion of Saints. Preeminent among all stands forth the Queen of Heaven — Mary, the ever blessed Mother of God; our Mother also, and the Refuge of Sinners. To her intercession we should ever have recourse; and we know that none has ever asked it in vain. But, after her, what better patron can we choose, if we be sinners — or if, being converted ourselves, we be praying for other sinners — than him whose whole life had been passed in iniquity, and yet whose conversion was so wonderful and so perfect that he was received the first into Paradise? When we read of his happy end we may say to ourselves: "Verily these things were written for our instruction." And we shall do well to beg of him to obtain for us a right understanding of them, and grace to imitate his repentance, as we have too surely copied him, in his revolt against God. And, if we continually keep his example before us, however much we may have sinned, we shall never be tempted to fall into despair. And let us make it a sacred duty to bring this example, as often as may be, to the minds of such as should, unhappily, have lost all hope in the mercy of God. And if, by the blessing of the Most High, we should succeed in opening, for this one ray of light, a passage to their souls, we may not doubt but that speedily the Day-Star shall arise, and the true Sun of Justice shine on them in all His splendor.

NOTES

CHAPTER 1

1 Epist. com. ad Episc. Mityl., t. viii.122.
2 Antiq. Jud., 1ib. xiv. c. ix. n. 2.
3 Joseph., Ant. Jud., 1ib. xx. c. v. vii. De Bell Civ., lib. ii. c. xii.
4 Ferraris, Bibllioth.Vo. Latrones.

CHAPTER 2

1 Eusebius, Hist., 1ib. i. c. xiii.
2 Epist. i., and deon. Isaur.
3 Apud Bar., an.769, n.8; an.809, n.17; an. 1181, n.17.
4 An. 1. n. 54.
5 Ibid., an. 48, n.14; an. 55, n.5; Index, t. i. p. 265-304.
6 Evang. Apocryph., p. v. vi. See also Bergier, Dict., art. "Apocryphes et Evangiles."
7 See Brunet, Evang. Apocr., p.54.
8 Ibid., p.53, etc.
9 Many of the Oriental writers say that Zoroaster was at one time a disciple of the prophet Elias. See a very interesting article (66 pages) on this subject by M. Parisot in vol. iii. of the Biographie Universelle. Zoroaster is by no means the only Gentile who has foretold events concerning the coming of the Desired of *all* nations.
10 The more wide-spread tradition gives them other names, but this is a mere detail. It is even very probable that they had several. Sacred as well as profane history furnishes many instances where the same personages were known under different names. Even to this day it commonly happens that robbers and other evil-doers find it convenient to drop their own name and adopt another under which they are less likely to be known or recognized.
11 De Vit. Eremit. Inter opp. S. Aug., t. i. p. 1380, edit. Gaume.
12 See Brunet, Evang. Apocryph. p. 102.
13 Serm. xliv., De SS. Innocent apud P. Orilia, p.10.
14 Catalog. II., lib. iii. c. ccxxviii.
15 Vita Jesu Christi.
16 Riflessioni, etc., c. ii. p. 10.

CHAPTER 3

1 Serm. vii., in Genes., p. 790, n. 5, opp. t. iv., edit. Gaume.
2 Serm. xlvi. de divers., in append.
3 De latra beat. In Bibl. Man., 66. t. v. 644.
4 De Cruc. et latr. Homil. ii.
5 Hist. Theologi. et moralis Terræ Sanctæ Elucidatio, I. ii.
6 Lieux Saints, t. i. c. xvii. p. 408.
7 Catalog. II., lib. iii. c. ccxxviii.
8 Riflessioni istoriche su la Vita del Glorioso San Dima, etc., c. xi. p. 11. This is a very rare book, printed at Naples in 1714. It has been approved and praised by ecclesiastical authority.

9   Evang. Apocr., ch. ix. p. 243, edit. Brunet.
10 Lib. iii. c. ccxxviii.
11 Serm. xliv. l. iii. de II. Innocent.
12 Tract xxxv., De Crucifix. Dom., t. x.
13 Hist. Theolog., etc., ut supra.
14 Act. Sanct. 25 Mart.
15 Metamorph. latro., c. i. a. 3 – Serm. x. in fine, c. xxi. – De. Sacr. Sind. – in Luc. lib. xiii. c. iii. – in Joan xvi., etc., id. Autor. Gislandus Quest. 677 in Dom. pass., etc.
16 De Cruce, lib. i. e. xii.
17 In Calig., c. xliv.
18 In Domit., c. l. The Parmularians were a portion of the infantry, so called from the shields they bore, named *parmæ*. The Mermilliones were a kind of gladiators who used to fight against the Thracians or the net fighters. They took their name from the image of a fish which they wore on the top of their Gallic helmets. – See Smith's Antiq., lib. i.
19 Ann., lib. i.
20 IX. Controv. ii.
21 In Sever., p. 64, edit. in fol. 1520.
22 Lamprid. In. Alexand., p. 186, edit. 1620.
23 Apolog., c. xliv.
24 Hist., lib. v. c. i.
25 "Foe of the Emperors and the Gods", Ad scapula., c. iv.
26 Salle des Martyrs, p. 333.

CHAPTER 4
1 Lips, De Cruce, lib. i. c. xii, Orilia, c. iii. p. 18.
2 Lamet, in Idyl, Allegor. Vis. Fin. Latro.
3 Serm. I. M. fer. V. Cæna Dom., t. v.
4 Moral, lib. xviii., c. xxiv-xxv
5 Apologet. S.S. Martyr. Cordulens
6 De Latrone beato, in Bibl. Man. P.P., t. vi, p. 614
7 De Laudib. Pauli.
8 Hist., lib. iv.
9 Satyr. vi.
10 Antiq. Rome, lib. v.
11 In Macr.
12 In Verr. V.
13 Dis. Hist., c. xii
14 De excid. Hierosol. lib. v. c. xxviii
15 Callist, J.C., lib. xxxvii, De Pænis.
16 Dissert. De Cruce, i. 573.
17 To the absence of the emperors from Rome may be traced the rise of the temporal power of the Popes, in itself essentially the triumph of the Cross. Whether or not, in its results, the gift deserved the epithet applied to it by Dante, is not for me here to discuss, but I may at least repeat, what has often been said by historians, Catholic and non-Catholic alike – viz., that, without it, Christendom would have been more than once overrun during the Middle Ages, and, both in its religious and political entity, not improbably done away with altogether. Idle to say, God might have found other means of preserving His Church. It would be blasphemy to doubt it. But, as a matter of fact, these were the means He chose. It is surely presumptuous to deny their having been the best admitted of by the circumstances of the world, at that time. – Tr.
18 See Gretzer, pp. 257-365.

19 Hist., lib. i.
20 Justin. Hist., lib. xxx.
21 Naler. Maxim, lib. ii. c. vii.
22 Corn. a Lapid., in Act. xii. 10.

CHAPTER 5

1 Since the above was written, this disgrace to English civilization has been done away with altogether, thanks to the humane and enlightened Government of Mr. Gladstone. – Tr.
2 Vid. Gallonio. De cruciat. S.S. Martyr, c. iv. S. Isidor. Etymol. lib. vi.
3 De pænis et ex lege Porcia.
4 Vide Cicero – Pro Rabirio. Valer. Maxim. lib. iv. c. i. Sigon, De antiquo jure Rom. lib. i. c. vi.
5 Baron. an. 34. pp. 83-84. Corn. a Lap. in Matth. xxvii. 26.
6 Ulpian. lib. viii, De pænis
7 According to the revelations made to St. Bridget, the number of these stripes mounted up to no less than 5,000.

CHAPTER 6

1 Lips., De Cruce, lib. xi. c. iv.
2 The reason may perhaps, be found in Pilate's desire to release our Lord. He thought that the lesser torment of scourging would satisfy the bloodthirsty hate of those who, for envy, had delivered Him, and that then, they would let Him go. This interpretation tallies with the words of St. Luke: "I will chastise him therefore and release him;" and further on: "But they cried again, saying, 'Crucify him, Crucify him.' And he said to them the third time: 'Why, what evil hath this man done? I find no cause of death in him. *I will chastise him, therefore, and let him go*'" (23:22). This same idea of saving the Just Man from death by means of tortures, which fell little short of it, seems to have had strong hold of Pilate. We find it again in that most touching incident of the *Ecce Homo*, recorded by St. John: "Pilate therefore went forth again and saith to them: 'Behold I bring him forth unto you *that you may know that I find no cause in him.*' Jesus therefore came forth bearing the crown of thorns and the purple garment. And he saith to them, 'Behold the man'" (19:4,5) – Tr.
3 Liv., Hist. lib. i.
4 De Sera Num. ira.
5 Omit., lib. ii. c. xli.
6 Antiq. Rom., lib. viii.
7 Hist., lib. iii.
8 De Divinat, lib. i.
9 Adv. Gent., lib. vii.
10 Dan. vii. 19.
11 Vid. Gretzer, De Cruce, lib. i. c. xvi.
12 This part of Italy bears today the name of The Marches.
13 Geograph. lib. v.
14 Aul. Gell., lib. x. c. iii.
15 Festus, vo. Brut.
16 De Corn. Milit, c. ii
17 See Baronius, an, 34, n. 33, 84.

CHAPTER 7

1 See Corn. a Lap., In Gen. xxii. 2.
2 Burchardus, Descript. Terræ. S. Genebrardus. Chronog., ib. i.
3 Serm. de S. Joan Bapt.
4 De rat. Temp., c. xlv.
5 See Mariana, De Rel. Hispan, c. xviii. 41
6 Dissert. 1, art. 7. De Doctr. temp, lib. xii. c. xi. See also Baron. an. 34, p. 153; and Sepp. Vie de N.S.J.C., t. ii. p. 387.
7 In some MSS., and notably in that preserved in the cathedral of Ephesus, which was said to be the autograph of St. John, the reading is different, and has, "about the *third* hour." (See Kenrick, The Four Gospels.) — Tr.
8 Const. Apost., lib. v. c. xiii.
9 Epist. Ad Trelleus.
10 The *scala sancta* have been removed to Rome, where they are exposed for the pious veneration of the faithful. No foot is allowed to touch these steps, made sacred by the Savior's tread. Those who would go up them must do so humbly, and on their knees — Tr.
11 The Sublime Porte has ever been a curse to such countries as have had the misfortune to fall under its dominion; but to-day it is an impotent anachronism. Yet its very weakness harms and corrupts that which it can no longer hold in check, just as an unburied corpse may infect the air, though it lack strength to defend the ground on which it lies decaying. Many reforms have been spoken of in connection with the Porte, but a Burials Bill is the only one like to prove effective. May it be brought in without much longer delay!– TR.
12 S.Greg. Moral. xix. 13.

CHAPTER 8

1 Apud. Corn. a Lap. In Gen. xxii. 2
2 Burckhardus, Descript. Terr. S., et Genebrardus, lib. 1. Chronograph. Apud eumd.
3 Lieux Saints, t. ii. c. xx. 39.
4 Descript. urb. Jerosol
5 Msgr. Gaume quotes this passage as being from Addison — "De la Relig. Chret., t. ii., and Lieux Saints, t. ii. c. xx. p.50, and c.i.p.25." The passage, however is not to be found in Addison's Discourse of the Christian Religion, which, I take it, is the work referred to under the French title given above. I have looked through his other works, but without finding any trace of the aforesaid incident. I am not aware that he ever wrote anything on the Holy Places. Possibly our author may have been mistaken in his reference. The story itself is well known. Maundrell is the name of the converted Deist. Not having been able to find the original passage, I have contented myself with simply re-translating Msgr. Gaume's version of it. – TR.
6 Apud. Andreas Masio. Josuæ imperat. Hist. illustrata atque explicata Antuerp., 1574, in fol., Comment. In Jos. c. ultim. P. 349
7 Massio, ut supra.
8 Gen.1.24. Exod. xiii.19. Joshua xxiv.32.

CHAPTER 9

1 Adv. Marcior., lib. 2. c. iv. p.1060, edit. Pamel. This rhythmical work, unfortunately little known, proves beyond doubt that Tertullian was as good a poet as he was a great orator and writer. It is much to be regretted that the admirable works of the fathers are not more known and read.
2 Origen, Tract xxxv. in Matt.
3 In Isaim. proph. c. v. n.141.

4   Hæres. xlv. n. 25
5   Tract. de Pass. Dom.
6   In Lucam. c. xxiii.
7   In Joan. Hom. lxxxv.
8   Serm. vi. De temp. n. 5. De Civ. Dei, lib. xvi, c. xxxii.
9   St. Cypr. De Resurrect. — Theoph. and Euphym. in c. xxvii. Matth.; Moses Ber Cephas — De Paradiso. Anast. Sinait., lib. vi. Hexæm. etc. Corn. A Lap. In Josue, c. ix., Baronius, an. 34, n.112. Gretzer, De Cruce, lib. i. xvii.
10 Adricomius, in Juda, n.7; see also the writers quoted by him.
11 Elucidat. Terræ S., lib. v. c. iv. p. 490.
12 In Matth. c. xxviii.
13 In Epist. ad Eph. c. v.
14 Epist. X. liv. Paulæ et Eustoch. aqd Marcellam.
15 Antiq. Jud., lib. v. c. ii.
16 Bar. An. 34, n.114, 115., Corn. à Lap. in ix. Jos., Melch. Canus. De Locis Theolog. lib. ii.
17 Albert. Magnus. ad xxiii. cap. Lucæ. Molanus, Hist. S.S. Imaginum. lib. iv. c. xi.
18 De Civit. Dei, lib. xvi. c. xxxiii; see also Corn. à Lap. in Gen. c. xxii. 2.

CHAPTER 10
1   Declam., 275
2   Lib. vi. c.ultim.
3   In Galb. c. ix.
4   Epist. ad Vincent. n. 43, opp.
5   Hist., lib. v. c. x.
6   Asin. aur. lib. vi. in fin.
7   Adv. Marcion, lib. iii. c. xxii.
8   In Ezech. ix. 4.
9   Epist. xxiv. ad Severum
10 In cap. xxii. Tertull. adv. Marcion. art. 174 p. 829.
11 Apud. Lable. Conc. t. ii. p. 133.
12 Hist., lib. viii. c. xxix.
13 In Clement De summa Trinitate. The Gloss is a celebrated mediæval commentary on the Holy Scriptures. The extract here given is quoted from the above-mentioned Treatise by St.Clement. — TR.
14 Ubi supra, p. 239.

CHAPTER 11
1   Artemid. lib. ii. c. lviii. Apud Lips, De Cruce, c. ix.
2   Enarrat. in Ps. cxviii., Tract. in Joan. xxxviii.
3   Hom. De Cruce et latr.
4   See all the authorities quoted by Molanus. De SS. Imag. lib. iv. c. x. De Nicephor. lib. viii. c. xxix. Theod. Hist. lib. i. c.xviii. Abulens. Paradox. Iii. c. xxxiv.
5   De Cruce, lib. i. c. ix.
6   Lucas Tudensis, lib. ii., Adv. Albigens. c. ii. Id. Greg. Tur. De gloria martyr, lib. i. c. vi. Bar an. 34 n. 118. Orilia, c. vii. Sandini, Hist., Fam. S. p. 218, etc.
7   Serm. i., De uno martyr.
8   See Gretzer, De Cruce, lib. i.c. i.
9   From the time of Calvin downwards much has been said to throw discredit upon the number of relics of the True Cross to be found in various parts of the world. The matter has lately been carefully investigated by M.Ch. Rohault de Fleury, who , after much

research, found that the aggregate size of all the relics known would amount (according to French cubic measures) to five millions of milimètres. Now this would have to be multiplied by 36 before reaching the total of 180 millions of milimètres (something about one-fifth of an English cubic yard), which calculations, based upon the best and most ancient traditions, give as the quantity of wood used for the Cross of our Lord. This would allow, consequently, of the existence of 36 times the amount of the portions of the True Cross which are known and authenticated; a very considerable margin, considering the smallness of the particles which are in the possession of private individuals, convents, and parish churches. See, for further information, M. de Fleury's very interesting Mémoire sur les instruments de la passion de N.S.J.C. — TR.

10 See Palat. Enarrat. In Joan. xix.
11 Lib. ii. c. lxxxviii.
12 In Joan. Tract. xxxvi. n. 4
13 Ut supra.
14 Ut supra.
15 Tit. Bostr. in Luc. xxiii.

CHAPTER 12
1 Orat. in Sepuler. Christi.
2 Lib. iii. De Adorat.
3 In Joan. Tract. xxxi. n. 11
4 Serm. iv. De Pass.
5 Serm. ii. De Pass. Dom
6 Serm. in Parasc.
7 Serm. v, in Dom. iii. Adv.
8 Serm. xlv. in append. Apud Orilia par. ii. c. i. p. 54.
9 "Abstulit iste suis cœlorum regna rapinis." Carm. v. Paschal.

CHAPTER 13
1 Catech xiii.
2 Moral., lib. xviii. c. xl.
3 In Luc. xxiii. 42.
4 See also St. Mark xiv. for evidence of St. Peter's indifference to the first crowing of the cock. True that neither St. Mark nor St. Matthew speak of our Lord's having looked upon Peter, but neither does St. John mention his conversion. Their silence, therefore, does no more to throw doubt upon the cause of conversion adduced by St. Luke than does that of St. John to discredit the fact of that conversion having taken place. – Tr.
5 Serm. ii. De Pass.
6 Tit. Bostr. in Luc. xxiii.
7 Joan. Carthag. De Sept. Verb
8 Serm. in Parasc.
9 In Act. v. 15
10 Apud Th. Raynald. Metamorph. c. iv.
11 Raynald. c. iv. p. 433 ita. Maldonat. in Matth. xxvii. 47. Toletus, in Joan. xix. annot. 9. Surarez. t. ii. pars. 3 disput. 40, etc.
12 Carm. Pasch., lib. v.
13 De Fide Orthod., lib. iv. c. xiii.
14 Lucas Tudens. Adv. Albigens. errores, lib. ii. c. xii. P. 226. – Biblioth.
    Max. P. P., t. xxv. In fol., Lugd. 1677. – See also Gretzer, De Cruce, lib. i. c. xxvi.

CHAPTER 14
1   Orilia lib. ii & vi, p. 107
2   In Ps. cxxvii. Exposit. n. ii. p. 431, opp. t. v., edit, Gaume.
3   De Cruce et latr. n. 2
4   1, 2 Quest art. 9. Cor.
5   Luc. Burgeu in Luc. c. xxiii.
6   S.G Magn., B. Albert Magn. In Luc. c. vii.
7   B. Albert. Magn., In Luc. vii., St.Bonavent. apud Sylveir. In Luc. vii., S. Ambr. in Luc. vii. B. Simon. De Cassia, in Luc. vii. apud Orilia, p. 97.
8   S. Bernard, De Pass. Dom. c. ix. Arnold. Carnot, De Sept. Verbis.
9   Orilia, p. 52.
10 St. Chrys. De Cruce et latr.
11 In Gen. Serm. vii. n. 4.

CHAPTER 15
1   St. Brun. De Ornament. Eccles. c.1.
2   De Cruce et latr. apud Orilia, p. 146.
3   De cœco. nato. opp. t. viii. p. 699
4   De cœco. nato. opp. t. viii. P. 699
5   See also Corn. á Lapide, in hunc. loc.
6   See St. August. Serm. clv. De Temp. in append. opp. t. v.
7   Homil. De Cruce et latr.
8   Serm. xliv. De Tempore, 2 Serm. clv. in append., id Enarr. in Ps. lxviii. Serm de fer. 3. Paschat., et De Anima, lib. i. c.ix.
9   Euseb. Gallic. Homil. de S. Latrone. Bibl Max. P.P.t.vi.644.
10 For reference to the principal passages of the fathers concerning the Good Thief, see Raynaldus and Orilia.

CHAPTER 16
1   Serm xxxvii.
2   Serm. 1 in Ps.xc.
3   De Pass.Dom.c. ix
4   Vitis Mystica, seu de Pass. Dom. c. ix. inter Opp. S.Bern.

CHAPTER 17
1   Moral xviii.13.
2   Serm. in Parasc. lv.c.11.
3   Homil. in Obit. Virg.
4   S. Max. Homil.1.De S. Latr.
5   S.Basil. Seleuc. Orat. in Bibl. P.P.
6   Vitis myst. c. ix.n.34.ubi supra.
7   B. Sim. de Cassia. in Luc. lib. xiii. De Pass c.iii.; also Chrys. De Cruce. apud Orilia,p.179.
8   In Lucam, xxiii. c. 6.

CHAPTER 18
1   Sum. I. Q. 57,a.3 ad. 4.
2   Orat. de 40 Martyr.
3   De Cruce et latr. n. 8.
4   De Pass. Dom.
5   Sum. I.Q. 61,a.4.
6   B. Albert. Magn. Parad. anim. lib. 1, c. x.
7   Serm. 10. De latronis salvatione, in Bibl. P.P.t. xxi.

CHAPTER 19

1   Sum. I.Q. 61 a 4.
2   De Morib. Eccles.cxv.
3   De quat Virt. Card.in fin.
4   Sum. ii. De Verb. Dom.
5   Sum. i.Q.61.
6   Pars iii. Concii.Sect.xliii.
7   Opera, Part iv. Termin. c. Fortitudo.
8   Opusc. v. Super Pater Noster petit 5.
9   Ugo a S. Char. In Epist. Jocob. Apost. c. iii
10 Godofr. Vindocin. Card. S.Prisæ. Serm. x. De S. Latr.
11 De Morib. Eccl. c. xxi.
12 Serm. xlv. De Venerat. S.S

CHAPTER 20

1   De Cæn. Dom. apud Orilia, p. 223; and Corn. à Lapide, in Lucam, xxiii.
    42. It is well known that, in the first centuries, the terms martyr and
    confessor were freely interchanged and considered almost synonymous.
2   De Anim. et ejus orig., lib. i.n.ii.opp. t.x., edit. Gaume.
3   Serm. cxx. De Tempore.
4   Epist. xiii. ad Paulin.
5   Lib. x.De Trinitate. See also Drogon. Ep. Ost., Tract de Sacram. Pass.
    Dom., Bibl. P.P.t.ii. P. Steph. Binet. De Bono Latr., etc.
6   Medit. in Pass. et Resurr. Dom. c. vi. Opp. t.v., edit. Gaume.
7   De Ira. iii.c.xviii.
8   In August. c. lxviii.
9   In Tib. c. lxiv.
10 Hist. lib. i.
11 Raynaldus c. xii.p.541. Baron. Martyrol. 7 April. Gretzer De Cruce, lib i.c.xxxii.p.88.
12 Tract 35. in Matth.
13 Ubi Supra.
14 Com. in Joan. xix.
15 Homil. xxii. in Evang.
16 Com. in Joan., c.xix.
17 Com. in Joan., xvi. Id. S. Anselm. Alloginum cœlest. xxx. Id. Joan. Carthagin. lib. ii.,
    De Christ., hom. iii. etc. etc.

CHAPTER 21

1   St. August., In Joan. Tract. xli. 1.3.
2   Luc. Burg., In Lucam, c. vii.
3   St. Ambros., In Psalm xl. We may observe from the passage that in the more ancient
    editions of the sacred text the word Amen was used twice over in the 43rd verse of the
    24th chapter of St. Luke's Gospel.
4   Arnold. Carnot., De. Sept. Verb.
5   Act. SS. Mar. et Marc. For a philosophical explanation of this religious phenomenon
    see St. Thomas, 3 p.g. 46, art 3. ad. 1.
6   Apud Navarin, In Luc xxiii. 287.
7   Vitis Myst. c. ix, inter Opp. S. Bernard
8   Ibid.
9   Arnold. Carnot., In Bibl. Max. P.P., t. xiii. part 4, p. 1266.
10 Alexand. de Hales, sup. Luc. xxlii. 51.
11 Epist. ad Dardan. n. 7.

12 De Cruce et Latr. n. 2.
13 *Vide* S. August. Serm. de diversis. 304. S. Eulog. Apologet. martyr Cordubens.

CHAPTER 22

1   S. Hier., In Matth. xxvii. 52.
2   De Myst. Christi. Quœst. liii. art. 3, n. 7.
3   S. Athan., Orat. De Pass. Dom., Origen, In Matth. Tract, 35. Alphons. à
    Castro, verb. Adam. Corn à Lap. In Gen. v. 5, etc. In Matth. xxvii. 53, etc.
4   Theoph. Raynald. Metamorph, etc., p. 555.
5   In Ancorato, etc.
6. See quotations from their writings in the "Bible de Vence." Dissertat. sur la résurr. des
    S.S. Pères. lxx. p. 185. Also Corn. à Lapide, In Matth. xxvii, 53, and Suarez, ubi supr.
    St. Thomas maintains and discusses both opinions, vid. 3 p.q. 53 art. 3 et. dis. 43 q. 1
    art. 3-9.
7   Hœres, 35 in fine.
8   Demonstr. Evangel. lib. iv. c. xii.
9   Metamorphos., etc. c. xiii. p. 554
10 Vid. Caten. aur., in Matth. xxvii. p. 372.
11 Corn. à Lapid. In Matth. xxvii, 53. Suarez ubi supr.
12 De Cruce et latr. n. 2.

CHAPTER 23

1   De Morib. Eccles. Cath. c. xv. n. 25; et Enarrat. 2 in Ps. xxxi. et passim.
2   St. Bernardin, Serm. li. fer vi., Post Dom. Oliv.
3   Ubi supra.
4   De caeco nato, ubi supra.
5   Serm. xliv., De Tempore.

CHAPTER 24

1   Serm. li. fer. vi. Post. Dom. Oliv.
2   Ubi supra.
3   Ubi supra.
4   Lib. xiii. c. iii.
5   P. 128.
6   St. Bernardine, ubi supra.
7   De Cruce et Latr.
8   In p. 2, 9, 24 – art. 3, iv. n. 3
9   II. 9, 24, art. 3.
10 St. Bern. Serm. de S. Benedict.
11 Ubi supra.
12 See Corn. à Lap., in Luc. xxii; i. 42.
13 De Sept. Verb.
14 St. Peter Damian, Serm. on St. Boniface.

CHAPTER 25

1. Our author here notes with approbation that this was the wise view taken nearly two
    thousand years ago of the question of capital punishment. On this, I must make two
    brief remarks: first, that I am not aware that even the wildest of modern philanthropists
    has ever suggested, in place of it, bribery as a means to justice, which seems to have
    been the only alternative deemed possible by Philo. Secondly — this is far too large a
    question to be so summarily dismissed — but in discussing it, it seems to me that the
    authority of a Hebrew writer, of whatever eminence, is of no weight, considering that

2 Philo. Lib. de Special, Leg.

3 This feast is kept on the 3rd of May, and is sometimes improperly called the *Invention* of the Cross, which, in the ordinary acceptation, is an obviously misleading rendering of the Latin *Inventio*, which should in this case be translated "discovery" or "finding." — TR.

4 De Cruce, lib. i. c. lxii. 192. St. Ambrosii, Orat. de obitu Theodos, Imp. S. Paulin., Epist. ad Sev., De invent. S. Crucis. Ruffin., Hist. Eccl. lib. l. c. vii., viii. Theodoret, Hist. Eccl., c. xvii. Alex. Monach., De Crucis Invent, apud Gretzer, lib. ii. p. 41, etc.

5 Nicephor., Hist., lib vii. c. xlix.

6 Suidas v°. Forum. Zonares, Annal, etc. Cedrenus, Compend. Hist. See also Gretzer, De Cruce, lib. i. c. xcix.

The law of force, which, in its time, rightfully exacted an eye for an eye and a tooth for a tooth, has long been done away with, and replaced by the higher law of love. By the standard of that law, and of that law alone Christians have to judge of the righteousness and expediency of inflicting the death penalty upon their fellowmen – TR.

CHAPTER 26

1 Serm. in Parasc., apud Gretzer, t. ii. p. 425.

2 Bolland. ad 25 Mart. Modern criticism affects to reject most of the traditions relating to the Good Thief. We would ask whether so much reasoning has had the effect of developing more reason among men? We think not.

3 Dies Iræ, verse xiii. See also St. Thomas' beautiful Eucharistic Hymn, *Adoro te devote,* verse iii:
"In cruce latebat sola Deitas,
At hic latet simul et humanitas;
Ambo tamen credens atque confitens,
Peto quod petivit latro penitens."   "On the Cross, the Godhead alone lay hidden, but here also is the Humanity hid: Nevertheless I believe in Both, and Both confess, and beseech Thee give what the Good Thief bought." – TR.

4 Euseb. Epis. Gall. – De Latrone beato – in Bibl. Max. P.P., vi. 644.

5 Ad Thod. Laps., Opp. t. i. p. 9, n. 6.

6 The Psalm here spoken of is the fiftieth, the *Miserere*, which is perhaps the most beautiful of those seven specially set aside by the Church for penitential purposes, as being fitted to excite in the breasts of sinners repentance, hope, trust, and love of God. – TR.

7 Enarrat. In Ps. 1, n. 3 et 5.

8 S. Chrysost., Opp. t. iii. 518. De Chananæa, No. 2.

9 Apud Bolland, Acta Sanct. In vita S. Porphyrii, 26 Feb. – T.